Sensus Communis

Sensus Communis

VICO, RHETORIC, AND THE LIMITS OF RELATIVISM

John D. Schaeffer

Duke University Press   Durham and London   1990

© 1990   Duke University Press
All rights reserved

Printed in the United States
of America on acid-free paper ∞

Library of Congress Cataloging-in-Publication
data appears on the last printed page of this
book.

For Laura

---

col dir pien d'intelletti dolci et alti,
coi sospiri soavemente rotti:
da questi magi transformato fui.
Petrarca

Contents

Acknowledgments

The publication of this book would have been impossible without the assistance and support of my wife, Laura J. Bird. Our conversations about Vico provided me with many crucial insights, and she criticized and edited the book's many drafts. She encouraged and humored me during many bleak hours. I count myself the most fortunate of men because my wife is my best friend and best colleague. I owe her whatever success this book enjoys.

I also owe a debt of gratitude to the National Endowment for the Humanities. I first became acquainted with the thought of Giambattista Vico at an NEH Summer Seminar in 1977. Later the Endowment supported my efforts with a one-year seminar in 1979–80 and a Fellowship for College Teachers in 1985–86. The Council for the Exchange of Scholars awarded me a research grant to Italy and Germany through the Fulbright Program in the Summer of 1983.

I wish to acknowledge the contributions of Charles H. Long, now professor of religion at Syracuse University, who directed those NEH seminars and who encouraged me to pursue Vico studies. I also wish to thank Giorgio Tagliacozzo, the director of the Institute for Vico Studies and editor of *New Vico Studies,* for his constant support and assistance.

I owe more than I can say to my teachers at St. Louis University: Walter J. Ong, S.J., my dissertation director, whose work on rhetoric and orality has provided my career with its agenda, and Clarence H. Miller, whose impeccable scholarship has long been my ideal, however distant I am from achieving it. Finally, I wish to thank my friends, Robert E. Jonas, David G. Schmidt and the late Richard L. Unger for their loyal support.

Chapter 3 grew from an article published in *Philosophy and Rhetoric,* "Giambattista Vico's Rhetorical Model of the Mind: *Sensus Communis* in the *De nostri temporis studiorum ratione*" (Summer 1981). Chapter 5 grew from an article, "*Sensus Communis* in Vico and Gadamer," in *New Vico Studies* (1987), and chapters 3 and 6 incorporate material published in "From Wit to Narration: Vico's Theory of Metaphor in its Rhetorical Context," in *New Vico Studies* (1984). I am grateful to the editors of these journals for allowing the use of these works.

Introduction

In 1953, Richard M. Weaver published a collection of essays, *The Ethics of Rhetoric,* that included "The Spaciousness of the Old Rhetoric." By "spaciousness," Weaver meant all that a nineteenth-century orator could take for granted, all the "uncontested terms" such as *freedom, valor, destiny,* and a host of others that could be invoked without fear of challenge, because the orator and the audience shared a common understanding of the terms' meanings. Weaver compared this shared understanding to capital and added: "If we knew how this capital was accumulated, we would possess one of the secrets of civilization. All we know is that whatever spells the essential unity of a people in belief and attachment contains the answer" (1953, 167). This "capital" is what I call *sensus communis,* and the story of how it is accumulated has been told by Giambattista Vico.

Vico was born in 1668 in Naples. He taught rhetoric at the University of Naples to students aspiring to enter the law school. As a true son of Italian civic humanism, Vico was imbued with rhetoric and convinced of its centrality to Western civilization. As a teacher of rhetoric, he characteristically conceived of thinking as occurring within an oral performance, and an extemporaneous performance at that. During his career Vico saw Cartesian rationalism challenge the three-hundred-year ascendancy of the humanist rhetoric he taught and loved. He responded by explicating the epistemology implicit in rhetoric. The key to that epistemology was what Vico called *sensus communis,* a term that means a great deal more than its English translation, *common sense.*

A proverb states that nothing is so uncommon as common sense, but what "common sense" has come to mean is not what Vico meant by *sensus communis.* A brief summary of those accrued meanings will clear the way for understanding what Vico meant by the term and why the concept may be of use to us now. *Sensus communis* has deep roots in Greek philosophy, where it has two different but complementary meanings. First *common sense* is frequently given as the translation for Plato's term *doxa*, the common opinion of the ordinary man. It means, in Platonic philosophy, hearsay or illusory knowledge built upon fleeting sense impressions. Its opposite is *episteme*, firm knowledge grounded in the forms and grasped through dialectical reasoning.

A second, more technical, meaning for *sensus communis* occurs in Aristotle's *De Anima*, where the philosopher attempts to account for how the human senses address themselves to individual things, for example, white objects, but still apprehend individuals as subsumed under universals (e.g., the category white) (426b8–427a15). In his commentary on the *De Anima*, St. Thomas calls this faculty *sensus communis* (I,q.1,a3,obj.2). Etienne Gilson summarizes the characteristics of this meaning of *sensus communis* as being (1) the common power that judges the acts of other senses; (2) the frontal root of all the senses; (3) that which perceives the objects of the external senses simultaneously, compares them, and appreciates their differences (1978, 32–33). For Aristotle and for Thomas Aquinas, then, *sensus communis* is an epistemological principle.

The Romans developed another meaning for *sensus communis* that emerged from the traditions of Roman stoicism. This usage occurs in Horace's satires (I, iii, 66) and in Seneca's *De Beneficiis* (I, xii, 3), where it means a sense of propriety, the shared but unstated mores of the community, the manners by which the community acts as a community. In short, the term means a conventional wisdom but with a decidedly ethical cast.

Descartes is the source of the most common meaning of *common sense* today: practical judgment. Common sense is what tells you to block the wheels of your car before trying to change a flat tire on a hill, or to carry an umbrella on a cloudy day. This meaning can be traced to the *bon sens* of Descartes, that elementary judging faculty that enabled people to follow his simple method of thinking. Because Descartes always argued that his method was practical for any reasonable person, good sense quickly became common sense.

Other Enlightenment philosophers returned to the Greek tradition of *sensus communis* and invoked common sense as a first principle on which the reflective and judging actions of the mind were based.

George Berkeley, David Hume, and Thomas Reid all used common sense as an epistemological principle that would keep the mind related to the external world and thus preserved from the skepticism of Cartesian rationalism.

By the eighteenth century *sensus communis* had become the locus of a whole cluster of meanings: an organizing sense, an unreflective opinion shared by most people, the manners or social values of a community, the first principle of reflection, an innate capacity for simple, logical reasoning. What Giambattista Vico did was synthesize the Greek and Roman ideas of *sensus communis*. The aim of this book is to show how he did it, and what this synthesis implies for current discussions of rhetoric and hermeneutics.

Vico's synthesis depends upon a "paradigm shift," but in this case it is, for us, a shift backward. I will show how Vico operated with an oral analogue for intellect, which he inherited from classical and humanist rhetoric, rather than with the visual analogue for intellect developed by Descartes with sources in Platonism. This book will therefore explore the significance of the orality implicit in Vico's *sensus communis* for rhetoric and hermeneutics.

In chapter 1 I sketch the history of rhetoric and show how the teaching of rhetoric gradually moved from an emphasis on oral performance to an emphasis on writing. This chapter differs from other histories of rhetoric, for example, that of George A. Kennedy, in that it focuses more on classroom practice than on the theories of major figures. In the second chapter I show how oral performance dominated the culture of Vico's Naples, and how that culture was under attack from the intellectual forces of the Enlightenment. The orality of Neopolitan life and the controversies over reform of the university and the legal system form the immediate context of Vico's career and thought.

Chapters 3 and 4 address Vico's writings and analyze the role of *sensus communis* in his thinking. In chapter 3 I examine Vico's writings on rhetoric and show how the simultaneity of invention, organization, and figurality that extemporaneous oral performance required became Vico's model for a holistic concept of *sensus communis,* which combined ethical and aesthetic judgment. Chapter 4 indicates how Vico's *New Science* developed this rhetorical idea of *sensus communis* into an epistemological principle that relates language to cultural development, and explains how *sensus communis* grounded Vico's version of cultural hermeneutics.

Chapters 5 and 6 are concerned with how Vico's idea of *sensus communis* contributes significantly to current discussions in hermeneutics and critical theory. Because Hans Georg Gadamer frequently refers to Vico and *sensus communis,* chapter 5 explores how Gadamer adapted Vico to his own hermeneutical system. I also explore the relevance of Vico's concept of *sensus communis* to the *Hermeneutikstreit* between Gadamer and Habermas.

The sixth chapter addresses the work of Jacques Derrida and places his thinking on metaphor and writing within the context of Vico's *sensus communis.* Derrida's work continues the Enlightenment's quarrel with metaphor and rhetoric, a quarrel that formed the context for Vico's thought. In this chapter I argue that Derrida's deconstruction of metaphor and privileging of writing is grounded in the visualist, even hypervisualist, analogue for intellect that French criticism has inherited from the Enlightenment. Vico's *sensus communis,* on the other hand, is grounded in an oral model for intellect and thus generates a completely different theory of metaphor and writing. Although Vico and Derrida begin at opposite poles, many of their conclusions are congruent.

In the conclusion I discuss the position of *sensus communis* with respect to some contemporary ethicians and rhetoric theorists. My point is that the arguments for ethical relativism emerge from the division between *sensus communis* as an ethical judgment and *sensus communis* as a linguistic consensus, precisely the division against which Vico argued and that his concept of *sensus communis* attempted to reconcile. I offer the writings of current philosophers such as Rorty, Bernstein, Williams, and MacIntyre as evidence of the attempt to rescue the first meaning of *sensus communis,* ethical judgment, and I present the work of theorists of rhetoric such as Richard Lanham as attempts to rescue the linguistic component of *sensus communis.* The philosophers, however, say nothing about the linguistic underpinnings of ethical consensus, nor do the rhetoricians address the ethical consensus that underwrites language.

Two philosophers, however, have addressed the impact of rhetoric on Vico's thinking, and their work forms the immediate background of this book. The first is Michael Mooney, whose *Vico in the Tradition of Rhetoric* (1985) painstakingly traces the various strands in the history of rhetoric from which Vico wove his thinking. The second is Ernesto Grassi, whose *Rhetoric as Philosophy* (1980) was the culmination of a career dedicated to establishing the philosophical respectability of the Italian humanist tradition. Grassi argued that Vico attempted to articulate the epistemological principles that underlay Italian civic humanism. He argued further that these principles, grounded in imagination and public life, gave Italian humanism the status of legitimate philosophy, but one different from—and in some cases opposed to—the German philosophical tradition that extended from Kant to Heidegger.

This book, however, differs from Mooney's and Grassi's in that I attempt to specify *sensus communis* as the concept that concretely relates Vico's thinking to the rhetorical tradition, and I specify *sensus communis* as an essentially oral concept that permits Vico to exfoliate the unity of rhetoric and ethics that characterized Italian humanism.

Sensus communis, Weaver's "spaciousness," is exactly what modern ethicians and rhetoricians find lacking. It is also what Gadamer and Derrida tell us we must challenge and, ultimately, do without. Vico not only tells us how the spaciousness came about, but also suggests the advantage of trying to reclaim it.

1 Orality and Writing in the
History of Rhetoric

ORALITY AND WRITING IN CLASSICAL RHETORIC

Until recently, the history of rhetoric in Western civilization has been treated piecemeal by many scholars. Two scholars, however, have attempted a broad interpretation of the history of rhetoric: Walter J. Ong has interpreted the tension between orality and writing in the Western rhetorical tradition, and George Kennedy has undertaken a magisterial investigation of rhetoric in each of the historical epochs of the West. In covering this vast canvas, Kennedy found it necessary to distinguish between rhetoric as using various arts and techniques in the creating of a discourse, and rhetoric as a cataloging and schematizing of those arts and techniques for teaching purposes. The first he calls "primary rhetoric," the other "secondary rhetoric." The latter is also susceptible to what Kennedy calls *letteraturizzazione,* transforming rhetoric into techniques of literary composition (1983, 17–19). Kennedy thus distinguishes between rhetoric as a rationale of speaking and rhetoric as a training program that may involve writing to a great extent. Kennedy's distinction allows us to trace in detail the shift in consciousness that Ong describes, the shift from an orally based consciousness and its attendant modes of thinking to a consciousness that has interiorized writing and altered its thought processes.

The work of Ong and Kennedy is critical in placing Vico within the history of rhetoric. Vico was aware of the distinction between primary and secondary rhetoric: he called effective speaking "eloquence"; "rhetoric" was the training by which one became eloquent. The distinction animates nearly all of Vico's writing, from his early inaugural orations at the University of Naples to the final version of the *New Science*. Vico also retained an acute awareness of the difference between orality and writing as modes of thinking. The first paragraph on "Principles" in the *New Science* (330) states that "for purposes of this study we must reckon as if there were no books in the world."[1] Certainly no study in modern times ever began with such an audacious demand upon its readers.

The difference between oral and written modes of thinking generated a tension in the history of rhetoric in the West, and Vico, in the eighteenth century, exploited this tension to the fullest, whereas the intellectual life of his time missed it completely. The tension must be traced if one wishes to understand Vico as the heir of the oral tradition because written, chirographic consciousness has assumed such ascendancy in our own time that the sources of Vico's thought in oral, performative rhetoric (or, as he would call it, eloquence) have been nearly silenced.

It is necessary to remind ourselves what it is like to live in a world without writing or print, to "reckon as if there were no books in the world," in order to understand what changes writing and print have accomplished. Ong has summarized the characteristics of oral culture (1982, 31–78). A brief review of those characteristics will show how orality conditions a culture and those who live within it.

The characteristics of oral culture derive from the qualities of sound itself. To be seen, something only has to exist, but to be heard, something has to make a sound. Sound denotes activity and frequently life; we suspect something is alive when we hear it making noises. In oral cultures a word is a happening. Words are not "objects" for the nonliterate; rather, they are transitory actions. Ancient Hebrew used the same word, *dabar,* to mean both *word* and *event* (Ong 1982, 32). The ancient Greek *logos* expressed a similar unity of word and happening.

Perhaps the most important fact about an oral culture is that the transitoriness of sound conditions that culture's knowledge. Without writing, a society can only know what it remembers orally, or to put it another way, it knows only what it can say aloud. Knowledge is structured to be recalled, and these structures comprise the forms in which oral cultures express their values. Such forms, however, are not extrinsic to the knowledge or values. Oral forms control the cultures' thinking; without them thoughts are unthinkable.

Two forms in particular are essential to oral retention of cultural knowledge: the formula and narrative. The former is really what makes the latter possible.

In an oral culture the tradition of the community must be continually re-presented in oral performance. Such performances have been studied by Milman Parry and Albert Lord (1954), who have pointed out that oral cultures need narrative plot lines—and memorable ones at that—to help organize the information necessary for the community's survival. The epic singer or storyteller brings to life the important traditions of the community. His or her songs and stories contain the cultural information the community needs to maintain its self-identity, and frequently such compositions contain a wealth of practical cultural information about manners, codes of behavior, or religious rituals. But such compositions are impossible to memorize verbatim the way a literate person memorizes the multiplication tables. The oral bard composes by having recourse to oral formulas, certain traditional expressions which, because of their meter, fit into certain places in a performance. The formulas not only provide metrical regularity, but also ideological continuity. For example, Homer's "man-slaughtering Hector" compresses Hector and the trait of killer into one compressed "character"; it is an epithet and also a judgment, a judgment the bard can maintain throughout the performance by simple repetition.

Besides narrative and its attendant formulas, there are other oral forms. The proverb encapsulates the collected wisdom of a community. It is revered because it is old and because it is anonymous: the product of the community itself. Or, in some instances, the proverb may be attributed to someone who had a reputation for wisdom, as the proverbs of Solomon. Whatever the ascribed authorship, the essential thing about a proverb is that it is memorable, that it expresses its lesson with some pithy image or sound effect. Another oral form akin to the proverb is the riddle. Oral cultures are fond of riddles because they can express a cultural value and also test the verbal acuity of the listener, making sure he or she is worthy of the wisdom.

In addition to being conditioned by oral forms, an oral culture's knowledge is also conditioned by the characteristics of oral performance itself. The most important of these characteristics is rhythm. Oral performance requires rhythmical, if not metrical, recitation, and information and narrative structure must fit rhythmical patterns.

Second, oral performance is necessarily repetitious. Not only formulas or plot structures, but even names and events are repeated constantly to keep them in both the hearers' and the singer's mind. Finally, oral performance is necessarily improvisatory. Even if the material has been recited hundreds of times, the singer will fashion it anew every time.

Orally controlled thinking is additive rather than subordinated. Oral cultures cannot structure knowledge into hierarchies of more and less important data. Likewise, oral thinking is aggregative rather than analytic: nonliterate thinkers can add new information to what they know, but they have difficulty in breaking down information into constituent parts. These two aspects of oral thinking, additiveness and aggregation, give rise to another: copiousness. As Ong points out, writing conditions us to think of thought as linear, proceeding in a straightforward chain of premises and conclusions pared of any extraneous matter (1982, 39). But for nonliterates, thinking is an exercise in perspicacity: the ability to relate as much as possible to the central issue. Nonliterate thinkers try to circumnavigate the issue, gathering in as much material as possible, trying to find every relevant proverb and story.

The perspicacity of nonliterate thought is grounded in another characteristic of oral culture: the constant reference of thinking to the concrete life of the community. Oral thought is never abstract in the way literate thought is. Oral thought is limited to *praxis,* what it is necessary to know in practical life (although the oral culture would consider a great deal "practical" that we might not, for example, stories about the origin of the tribe will have clear practical implications about certain rituals). For this reason, oral thought is naturally conservative. Its primary task is cultural transmission, not cultural innovation. Even when circumstances force a new social reality on a culture, the storytellers will interpret that reality in terms of received traditions and present it as continuing the group's traditional values and sense of reality.

Although oral thought tends to be conservative, it is never univocal. Oral thinking is characterized by conflict; it is what Ong terms "agonistically toned" (1982, 43). Because oral thinking always occurs within a context of praxis, and within a context of public performance, it is perforce argumentative. Writing fosters detachment and abstraction; orality fosters involvement and debate. Oral cultures are usually characterized by some tradition of "flitting," ritual name-calling and insults. On the other hand, oral cultures frequently institutionalize rituals of praise and glorification. Such practices are understandable when one remembers that, without writing, there is no "past" lying outside of the spoken word that can render judgment on the correctness of a decision or the virtue of a person. The judgment of one's contemporaries remains constant so long as it is repeated in maxims or narrative; if that judgment changes, then the narratives must be recast.

Oral culture remains in a kind of constant present by deliberately forgetting things that are no longer important to practical life. Words themselves only have meaning within the context of spoken articulation, a context controlled by gesture, audience, and many other extrinsic factors. The relation of words to other words is problematic in an oral culture. It is not unusual for oral cultures to use ancient language or words in certain physical contexts, like drum-talk or epic recitation, which are otherwise totally neglected (Ong 1982, 47–49).

Ong's description of what oral culture is like concludes with two extremely pregnant observations: first that oral cultures have what he calls a "verbomotor" life-style, and, second, that oral culture is characterized by sound's ability to incorporate or to unify disparate elements (1982, 68–74). By "verbomotor life-style," Ong means a culture's dependence on words to achieve its transactions rather than on things. The sort of dueling that goes on in open-air markets in the Mediterranean, the haggling and bargaining, is verbomotor and contrasts with the cool material exchanges that occur in a supermarket in a Western, or westernized, country. A verbomotor life-style features the aggression, the value of tradition, and the practical-mindedness of oral culture. Oral culture also is imbued with the unifying power of sound. Sound comes from all sides at once; it is simultaneous and, at the same time, produced by something that may have an interiority. Vision objectifies and isolates, hearing subjectifies and merges us with sound. Sound can breach the frontier of the self, the body, and enter us in ways no other sense data can. Hence, oral culture is both more communal and more vulnerable than literate culture; its participants not only feel more togetherness, but also feel more threatened than those of literate cultures.

Ong's description of oral culture is critical to understanding the tradition of rhetoric in Western culture. Rhetoric was the first attempt to systematize the skill of oral speaking, that is, to claim that successful participation in an oral culture was a skill that could be learned. Rhetoric participated in all the qualities of orality that Ong has outlined: its agonistic quality, its dedication to public life, its dependence on formulas and memorization, and its assumption of the sort of verbomotor life-style that characterizes oral culture. Yet rhetoric was impossible without writing.

Writing provided both the practical and theoretical preconditions for the emergence of an art of speaking. Primitive, nonliterate cultures frequently have "rhetoric" in the sense of prescribed modes of address and ceremonial speeches. But such activity is really "formulaic speech" and follows the cultural and linguistic patterns first studied by Parry and Lord. Classical rhetoric, on the other hand, purported to inculcate a skill in public speaking on any subject in a variety of social contexts. In short, rhetoric claimed to be an art that could employ language as a tool to achieve a variety of ends. At this level, language itself is objectified, abstracted from any concrete, specific social situation, and this level of abstraction requires writing, and even in some respects a phonetic alphabet.

The most obvious function of writing in an "art" of rhetoric is to make accessible the figures of speech, the tropes and schemes. Although on the one hand it is certainly not necessary to be able to write to use such figures, or even to abstract them from a particular discourse, on the other hand, to name them, catalog them, and teach them independent of a particular speech require that they be written. Although a rhapsode may have known all the formulas in the *Iliad,* he had to sing it to remember them; it is unlikely he could have recited a list. Even if he could, he could never have taxonomized them by type such as metaphor or metonymy. In short, rhetoric as an "art" requires the construction of what we now call "second order discourse," and such discourse is beyond the reach of a mind that operates exclusively in oral formulas.

But writing is also necessary for rhetoric in another, deeper way. While writing allows for a decontextualization of individual utterances, it also allows for an objectification of discourse in larger scales. The process of *dispositio,* for example, presupposes that a discourse can be divided and subdivided into parts, and those various parts of one speech seen as species of genres of parts. To see that one of Cicero's speeches begins with a proem implies that a "proem" exists apart from Cicero's speech. Furthermore, to find and discriminate such parts requires dealing with a discourse as a whole, that is, conceptualizing it as all existing at once, as if on paper, even if it really is not written down. The mental operation required to conceptualize rhetoric as an art of speaking implies writing; only through writing is discourse made available for the sorts of genus/species divisions that generate rhetoric as an "art."

Ancient Greece is generally agreed upon as the birthplace of rhetoric, and we can see in that birth the origins of the tension between the oral milieu for which rhetoric supposedly prepared its students and the chirographic milieu that made rhetoric possible.

Studies by T.B.L. Webster and J.W. Roberts have described the intensely oral milieu of Athens in the fifth century B.C. An Athenian citizen was responsible for defending himself in court against criminal or civil charges, and lawsuits occurred with a frequency that even the most litigious twentieth-century American would find dismaying. Juries were huge by contemporary standards, frequently in the hundreds, and the average Athenian could expect to spend a good part of his life serving on them. Court business was transacted orally; plaintiff and defendant pled their cases usually on very short notice, sometimes only a few hours (Roberts 1984, 56–60).

In addition to court appearances, public speaking was the primary mode of conducting most business. Recruiting troops, declaring wars, forming alliances, establishing colonies, and every other conceivable government act was decided on in the course of public debate before an audience of the citizenry. The stakes in such debates, just as in the law courts, were high. The loser could face disgrace or exile. And, finally, public speaking served as the knot maintaining a whole network of community relations. No festival or celebration was complete without a speech praising the values of the society and pitying or contemning those of others. Ability to speak effectively at best guaranteed access to the public life of the city; at the very least it was essential to defend oneself from exploitation or victimization at the hands, and voices, of neighbors.

The struggle between orality and chirographic thinking can be traced as far back as Plato's controversies with the Sophists. In those controversies we can see how, in the guise of struggling over mere pedagogy, two sorts of thinking struggled over the status of truth itself.

The Sophists accepted the values and habits of the oral milieu of Athens as normative, but they saw themselves as increasing the "social efficiency" of the city's life (Beck 1964, 171). Their educational program assumed citizens to be social beings and to succeed in the life of the polis meant assenting to and participating in the moral consensus that formed and sustained the polis. The "good man" in sophistic educational theory conformed to his polis's mores and could appeal to them to foment his own ends and advance his own status (Jaeger 1965, 286–91).

The educational practice of the Sophists was fundamentally oral.[2] They were the heirs of the tradition of the rhapsodes, and their teaching methods adapted the techniques of oral poetry to public speaking. The Sophists saw the orator as a politically involved rhapsode, creating speech out of traditional materials and arranging them to achieve a particular end in a concrete situation. These traditional materials were learned in the exercises with which sophists began their educational program: the *progymnasmata*. These were anecdotes, fables, pithy sayings, and stories arranged in ascending order of difficulty; they were the Sophists' invention and were to remain a part of elementary literary education for 2,500 years.

The Sophists' educational program involved memorizing these commonplaces, formulas, figures of speech, and stock phrases, along with larger units of discourse: model orations that contained many figures of speech, for example, the funeral oration of Gorgias, which was intended to be a compendium of such formulas. Writing was used only as an aid to memory. After committing such passages to memory, the student would be called upon to improvise an oration on the spur of the moment. These extemporaneous performances could be on either side (or even on both sides) of a hypothetical question, and this exercise was performed constantly, giving the young orator a facility in speaking ad hoc in the public forum. The exercises, in one form or another, were to remain the backbone of rhetorical education until the nineteenth century, and they contributed no small part to the popular opinion that equates rhetoric with sophistry.

Today we admit that there was far more to the Sophists than we see in the caricatures in Plato's dialogues. Yet the term *Sophist* remains one of contempt and indicates how deeply Plato's views have permeated our consciousness.

Within the past three decades scholars have sought the roots of Plato's attack on sophistry in the emergence of literacy. Eric Havelock has argued (1963) that Plato was the first Western philosopher to have interiorized writing, that is, Plato was the first Western philosopher to conceptualize thought as writing. He "thought writing" as opposed to the Sophists and most members of Athenian society who thought talking: characteristically conceived their own thinking within a model of oral performance. The difference between Plato and the Sophists was not a philosophical difference of opinion, it was a difference in modes of thinking itself, modes shaped by different media, producing different analogues of intellect and implying different social values.

Socratic method, in Plato's hands, challenged the oral mode of culture as well as its received values and meanings. Socrates insisted on reflection, not inspiration, personal private interviews rather than public performances, and, most important, dialectical interrogation rather than debate based on shared values. Plato actually portrays this tension in the *Protagoras,* and in the *Phaedrus* Plato illustrates the peculiar paradox of oral and written modes of thought in ancient Greece. In it, Socrates remarks that writing is inferior to speaking because writing will hinder the memory—but Plato wrote that down.

Just how radically Plato parted company with the Sophists can be seen by comparing Plato's educational program with that of the Sophists who trained young men for participation in democratic government. Plato's educational system aimed at creating a ruling elite. The Sophists emphasized verbal memory, aiming to provide their students with maximum linguistic resources. Plato emphasized visual, sequential reasoning aimed at liberating his students from the imprecision of language by training their minds to operate formally, especially through practice in mathematics. Most important, the chief mode of sophistic training was the impromptu speech, whereas students at Plato's academy *wrote* dialogues (Beck 1964, 233–39). Sophistic training imbued its students with an ad hoc theory of reasoning, one controlled by *kairos,* the immediate situation, the present audience. Plato's academy, on the other hand, featured dialectic, the interrogation of meaning in give-and-take aimed at arriving at conclusions independent of the opinions of the interlocutors and independent of any transient social or political condition. Such a view disincarnates language from its social context, and the academy found writing and mathematics to be the best training for its purposes and, following their master, found that written representation of dialectic was superior to the actual conversation. The representation achieved its effect upon a reader perhaps more tellingly than actual dialogue did upon a listener.

The Platonic academy was the first institution to develop an entire educational program based on writing. The contrast between the Sophists and the Platonists operated in Western culture to the time of Vico and continues to the present. This contrast is more than just a difference in educational programs. It involves polarities that control much of Western philosophy: words versus things, democracy versus aristocracy, persuasion versus demonstration, poetry versus mathematics, and—I would argue—orality versus visualism as analogues for conceiving intellect. Other educational theorists arose in Athens, for example, Isocrates and Xenophon, with programs that tried to adjudicate between or transcend the difference between rhetoric and dialectic, but the difference was too profound, rooted in a shift of consciousness at the deepest level.

To see how deep this tension permeated, one need look no further than Aristotle. His work on rhetoric was by far the most influential in the Western rhetorical tradition, and it is worthwhile to see how it encapsulates the tension between the oral tradition of the Sophists and the chirographic mentality of his mentor, Plato.

Frederick Solmsen has argued that Aristotle's *Rhetoric* is actually a Platonic work that taxonomizes emotions and the ways in which they can be appealed to, thus fulfilling the proposal for a rhetoric addressed to the "forms of souls" made in the *Gorgias* (1965, 131). In any event, there is no doubt that Aristotle, in the *Rhetoric,* regards his subject with suspicion: "But we must not forget that such things [rhetorical techniques] are, every one of them, extraneous to a speech. They are for the audience, an audience that is weak enough to accept utterances beside the point" (1415b). The "point," of course, is the argument, that which can be structured dialectically: "What is true and preferable is by nature always easier to prove, and more convincing" (1355a). Aristotle assumes a "natural" correlation between proof and truth and further between truth and conviction: what is "true" will be convincing—naturally.

Aristotle proceeds to taxonomize rhetorical propositions, that is, propositions proper to persuasive speech rather than to strict demonstration. He is concerned with probability: How can people be convinced of the truth of something that is in fact only probably true? A proposition is probably true when its major premise is only probably true. Aristotle calls such a proposition an *enthymeme*, for example, "Since war is inevitable, we must be prepared." The inevitability of the future can only be probable, hence the whole proposition can be only probably true. Aristotle tries to taxonomize the sorts of enthymemes. The result is the *topoi*, the list of "places" from which arguments can be drawn.

Later in the *Rhetoric* Aristotle taxonomizes the figures of speech, metaphor, synecdoche, and irony. Once again, he wishes to arrive at an empirical account. He carefully distinguishes simile, symbol, and metaphor, the latter being, strictly speaking, a proportional figure: *A* is to *B* as *C* is to *D*. He gives examples of each figure, many from poetry. But each is presented as a variation on a propositional statement. The implied lesson is that these figures are ways of approaching the mind through the passions, but that it would be better if argument could be stated "naturally," that is, in syllogisms.

The real tension in Aristotle's *Rhetoric* is between audience-centered performance and a fact-centered dialectic. When dealing with arrangement, Aristotle implies that logic alone ought to be sufficient for conviction—what Richard Lanham calls the "Edenic view" (1983, 15–23). As Aristotle says: "A speech has two parts. You must state your case, and you must prove it. . . . Of these two parts the first part is called the statement of the case, the second part the argument, just as we distinguish between problem and demonstration" (1414a30–36). Yet Aristotle proceeds to adopt the usual four-part division of the oration on the grounds that the audience's weaknesses require it. What Aristotle finds uncomfortable are those things the audience requires. In fact, he finds the audience uncomfortable. One gets the impression that Aristotle would cheerily dismiss them from his mind, because their presence contributes nothing but the disfigurement of a dialectic that ought to be exclusively focused on facts.

Aristotle's *Rhetoric* was the text of secondary rhetoric in Europe for centuries. It provided the apparatus for teaching the various parts of rhetoric and gave its readers a substantial catalog of figures and schemes, as well as the standard list of the *topoi*. Yet this impressive achievement was impossible without writing and, in fact, the very Platonic training that made it possible called into question its value as an educational tool. Aristotle clearly believed that the oral culture for which rhetoric was designed would be better served by dialectic, that is, by thought processes made possible by the interiorization of writing. In short, secondary rhetoric is accompanied by the emergence of thought processes which invalidate the oral culture that thrives on primary rhetoric.

Greek rhetoric was situated in the persons of individual teachers such as Isocrates, or theoreticians like Aristotle. It never developed into a national system. That development was reserved for Roman rhetoric. Rome adapted Greek rhetoric and made it a coherent educational *disciplina*. Just as the tension between oral and written modes of thought is most evident in Greek rhetoric, so in Roman rhetorical training we have the most comprehensive reconciliation of those tensions, although it is a reconciliation that favors orality. Vico saw himself in the Roman, not the Greek, rhetorical tradition. Thus it will be beneficial to review the characteristics of Roman rhetoric in some detail.

Roman rhetoric was situated at the end of an educational process. Although Roman pedagogy did not differ in many ways from that of the Greeks, it did differ in that the Romans formed a self-consciously incremental system, and its last step was rhetoric. In Greece rhetoric was taught by itinerant Sophists who frequently hawked their wares by promising a short-cut to eloquence. In a certain sense Rome did for rhetoric what Plato had done for dialectic: it marshaled an educational procedure to aim toward it.[3]

Roman rhetoric displays the tension between oral and chirographic values in a systematic fashion. The pedagogy and educational philosophy of Roman rhetoric structured that tension into an educational package that became the model of education for Western Europe from

Roman times until the rise of medieval logic, and again from the Renaissance until the twentieth century.

Greek language and educational practices arrived in Rome in the second century B.C., and they remained together until the fall of the Empire. Primary education in Rome meant learning Greek and Latin simultaneously. Greek was a sine qua non of advancement in grammar and rhetoric. Of course, early Greek teachers met with the usual Roman xenophobia, but eventually Greek won acceptance as a cultivated literary language and also as the lingua franca of the Mediterranean world. Roman rhetoric was "humanistic" in that it taught a second language viewed as culturally superior to the native language of the students.

The Roman education system has been studied by Stanley F. Bonner (1977), who points out one aspect of Roman bilingual education that is connected intimately with writing. To teach young boys Greek required considerable writing, and classroom papyri still exist showing how students laboriously copied nouns and verbs to master Greek inflections. By the same token, however, similar exercises were used to inculcate correct latinity. Spoken, idiomatic Latin was shaped into a rather regular system by the *grammatici,* the Roman grammar teachers. There was apparently a wide discrepancy between vulgar Latin and the Latin taught at the schools (Bonner 1977, 189–211). Roman education valued "correct" Latin early on, and correctness was derived by modeling Latin grammar on Greek grammar in ways that required writing for its mastery. In other words, rhetorical training in Rome was founded on an elementary education that attempted to control Latin chirographically. From its origins, Roman grammar aimed to teach boys to speak correctly, that is, to "talk writing." But writing was for talking.

The grammar schools retained many of the values Ong describes as characterizing oral culture. The schools were called *ludi,* that is, play-areas, the same word that was used for the fields where martial exercises were performed. The teacher was known as the *magister ludi,* the master of the contest (Bonner 1977, 56–57). The instruction of grammar school students involved three processes: copying in writing, memorization, and recitation. The teacher would dictate a passage, almost always from poetry, and the students would copy it, memorize it, and then recite it to the class. These recitations featured not merely "literal" recitations of the words. The students were to concentrate on rhythm, correct meter, and pronunciation. The teacher would frequently accompany recitations, his own and students', by drumming his fingers or stamping his foot to set the proper rhythm. In addition, the grammar schools developed a whole set of diacritical marks to enable students to "see" the correct pronunciations and rhythms on their tablets or papyri. Writing was practiced continually in class by copying *sententiae,* witty, pithy, or proverbial sentences that were memorized in large numbers. Lists of them have come down to us, and, in fact, they play a very important role in Renaissance rhetoric and in Vico's thought. But in Rome, students first made their acquaintance with *sententiae* as subjects for memorization and constant copying.

As students progressed, the passages they memorized and copied got longer. Long passages of Homer in Greek and Virgil in Latin were copied, memorized, and recited. Other authors frequently used included Menander, Euripides, Horace, and Terence. The dramatists frequently supplied precedents for grammatical or syntactical usage, because their works were written down with care (Bonner 1977, 204–8). Grammar students were indoctrinated in the most literal sense of the term: memorizing and reciting long passages of poetry that embodied national and cultural values. Here we see the characteristic conservatism of oral culture. At higher levels of instruction teachers would comment on the poems, parse and construe difficult passages, and begin pointing out and explaining figures of speech. But in grammar classes, the students' responsibility was internalization of texts and their faithful recitation.

The most popular form of such recitations was the speech "in character." The student memorized a speech given by a particular person and then "acted it out." Dido's speech on her funeral pyre, from the *Aeneid,* was a particular favorite. Frequently, however, the speech had to be extemporized with appropriate gestures, sometimes even in verse. The performance emphasized not only a correct literal memorization, nor even correct enunciation of the words and their quantities in proper meter, but also how the emotion displayed by the student suited the words and sense of the passage. The speech "in character" was instruction in drama; the student had to replicate the emotion of the character in his performance in a way that was convincing. The student had to "put on" Dido and impersonate her. This means he first had to discover the sort of emotions and passions proper to her situation and then to express them within the strict limits of the verse and its meter. This exercise, more than any other, recaptured the spirit and practice of the bards. At a more practical level, oral performance of the speech "in character" gave the young orator an experience of how people feel in certain situations and how they behave when they so feel. Rhetorical instruction, like drama, involved "acting" and left rhetoric open to the charge of insincerity that bedeviled it from Plato to Pascal.[4]

After training in reciting memorized passages of verse and prose, the student moved from these rote recitations to the *progymnasmata*. These exercises were the same as those taught by the Greek rhetors, although Roman rhetors were sometimes content to let the humble *grammatici* teach them while they saved themselves for the declamation. Unlike the Greek rhetoricians, however, Roman rhetoric required the student to write, memorize, and recite passages of his own composition in both prose and verse in increasing levels of difficulty. These passages were imitations of those he had been copying, memorizing, and reciting for years, a process that ensured that the student had a ready stock of models already memorized.

After concluding the *progymnasmata* the student moved to the study of rhetoric and its proper form, the declamation. Once again, the student was expected to write out his speech, memorize it, and then declaim it before the class and any visitors who happened to be present. The declamation took either of two forms: the *suasoria,* a deliberative speech, or a *controversia,* a forensic speech on a hypothetical case. The *suasoria* continued the student's "dramatic" training, for in it he had to impersonate someone who was advising a king. Thus, even the declamation was "performed" in a dramatic context in which the student had to "put on" some character. In the *controversiae,* the most frequently debated issue, both in schools and in court, was the "letter" of the law versus the intent of the legislators. The tension between writing and speaking was enshrined self-consciously in this particular exercise. Such exercises trained the student for speaking in courts as well as in deliberative assemblies such as the Senate.[5]

The declamation was usually prepared beforehand, but the original intent of the declamatory exercises was preparation for extemporaneous speaking, as Quintillian testifies:

> But the crown of all our study and the highest reward of our long labours is the power of improvisation. The man who fails to acquire this had better, in my opinion, abandon the task of advocacy and devote his powers of writing to other branches of literature. . . . For there are countless occasions when the sudden necessity may be imposed upon him of speaking without preparation before the magistrates or in a trial which comes on unexpectedly. And if any such sudden emergency befalls, I will not say any innocent citizen, but some one of the orators' friends or connexions, is he to stand tongue-tied and, in answer to those who seek salvation in his eloquence and are doomed, unless they secure assistance, to ask for delay of proceedings and time for silent and secluded study, till such moment as he can piece together the words that fail him, commit them to memory and prepare his voice and lungs for the effort. (Quintillian, X, vii, 1–2)

Roman rhetoric during the Republic and early Empire was decisively oral, moral, and ludic. The educational system preserved much of the values of oral culture. It featured memorization and recitation and used writing as a propaedeutic to those. Futhermore, the material copied and memorized and recited was heavily laden with proverb lore and purple passages that indoctrinated the young grammar student with culturally approved values in a manner reminiscent of the conservatism of oral culture. The education was ludic in that it featured competition: rewards and applause for success; shame and even corporal punishment for failing to make the grade, preserving the "agonistic tone" of oral culture. Furthermore, rhetoric training was theatrical, emphasizing oral delivery and interpretation. The ultimate objective of the whole system was to produce speakers capable of successful extemporaneous forensic declamation. Like the Sophists from whom it borrowed so much, Roman rhetoric was essentially civic-minded and culturally conservative. In the Republic and early Empire, secondary rhetoric was geared toward primary rhetoric—extemporaneous oral performance.

The formalization of secondary rhetoric, its *letteraturizzazione,* or incorporation into detailed and structured texts for use in literary composition, was completed in the Eastern empire in the period known as the Second Sophistic. There, according to Kennedy, extemporaneous speaking disappeared (1983, 7–19). Courtroom pleading was replaced by a process of formal inquiries and petitions which were communicated in writing. Oral performance was restricted to ceremonial declamations, written, memorized, and then pronounced before an audience. These performances were held on nearly all state occasions and were, in fact, a chief mode of imperial propaganda. But, in general, rhetoric in the Eastern empire was a course of study aimed at conformity to inherited canons of propriety and diction more than a preparation for extemporaneous speech in public situations pregnant with controversy.

The rhetorical culture of ancient Rome endured with many permutations until well into the early Middle Ages, but one man retrieved it from formalism and adapted it to the Christian culture then emerging in the West: Augustine. His approach to Christian and Jewish scripture and their interpretation reconstellated the relation of language, text, and speaking within the matrix of Christian theology. This reconstellation has had profound implications for the way subsequent Western culture has seen rhetoric and its relation to writing and orality.

ORALITY AND WRITING IN LATE ANTIQUITY AND THE MIDDLE AGES

C. S. Baldwin said that Augustine's *De doctrina christiana* "begins rhetoric anew" (1928, 51). Augustine saw that the tradition of classical rhetoric could and should be used to preach the gospel. As a rhetor himself he knew the advantages that his training conferred, but at the same time he also knew the kind of applause-seeking vanity with which the rhetoric of the Second Sophistic was infected: its striving after effects, its canons of diction and decorum, and, above all, its lack of any meaningful controversy in which to be effective. Christianity offered Augustine a new sphere for rhetorical activity, one entirely different from the pagan empire, and he adapted rhetoric to it.

Augustine himself was intensely oral, and he returned to rhetoric's original emphasis on extemporaneous speaking. He could not read silently; he always read aloud. In a well-known passage in the *Confessions,* he relates how he saw Ambrose standing silently before a book. When a servant told him that Ambrose was reading, Augustine was incredulous because he could hear nothing *(Confessions* 133–34).[6] He devotes the first three books of the *De doctrina christiana* to the proper understanding of scripture, and it is clear that "understanding" means understanding the text to put the correct meaning into an oral reading: "he who teaches how the Scriptures are to be understood is like a teacher who advises how the words are to be read" *(De doctrina* 7). When discussing the style of the scriptures, Augustine refers to its sound; his discussion of periodicity, for example, features delivery, how the period should be read aloud (149 f.)

Augustine's oral approach to reading extends also to preaching. His model of preaching is audience-centered and extemporaneous: "an attentive crowd eager to comprehend usually shows by its motion whether it understands, and until it signifies comprehension the matter being discussed should be considered and expressed in a variety of ways. But this technique may not be used by those who have prepared what they have to say and memorized it word for word. As soon as it is clear that the audience has understood, the discourse should be finished or another topic taken up" (134–45).

Augustine restored the oral, extemporaneous, performative quality of rhetoric and imbedded it in the Christian *ars praedicandi.* His master in this restoration was Cicero, but he made several changes in Cicero's rhetoric: the three objectives of eloquence—to teach, to delight, to move—became, in Augustine's theory, the three successive stages of preaching. The three styles—the low, middle, and high—were to be determined by the objectives of the preacher, and all three could be employed in one speech. For Cicero, the styles were determined by the subject matter, and the style controlled the whole speech. These were profound changes in classical rhetoric, but, nonetheless, Augustine's impact was more restorative than innovative. While the empire had formalized rhetoric during the Second Sophistic, Christian preaching opened a new theater for extemporaneous oral performance, and Augustine reached back to the tradition of republican rhetoric and brought it to bear on Christian preaching. In doing so, he shaped Christian preaching and thought for the next seven centuries.

The centuries we call the Middle Ages saw another process of *letteraturizzazione* analogous to that which characterized the Second Sophistic. The oral, performative rhetoric recaptured by Augustine was textualized as secondary rhetoric and eventually reduced to mechanical techniques of literary composition. Medieval rhetoric, according to Richard McKeon, has no history at all (1965, 212). Rhetoric was identified with, or assimilated to, logic and grammar. Yet the existence of a medieval art of preaching *(ars praedicandi),* as well as an art of letter writing *(ars dictaminis)* and a concern with writing verse *(ars poetriae),* argues that something was happening in the Middle Ages that we would call rhetoric. What did happen was that, while rhetoric as an educational *disciplina,* in the sense in which Aristotle and Cicero used that word, did not exist, parts of rhetoric were mixed with logic and grammar to form methods of teaching particular forms of discourse. More significantly, however, the practice of extemporaneous oral performance was continued, but under the aegis of logic, not rhetoric. The *disputatio* replaced the declamation as the premier performative mode, yet it, too, was subject to a kind of *letteraturizzazione.* The process by which all this happened further illustrates the way textualization transforms rhetoric.

Latin was transmitted through the grammar school, and it was here that the first of the medieval arts, the *ars poetriae,* began. Because the medieval grammar schools aimed at preserving Latin, the *ars poetriae* was developed to assist in *writing* Latin poetry. The days of extemporaneous Latin poetic performance were over. Furthermore, the manuals of the *ars poetriae* were directed toward discovery, order, and wording to encourage the imitation of textual models. The *ars poetriae* was developed to make the writing of Latin poetry conform to certain canons. To this extent it reflects the conservative impetus of medieval grammar. After 1200, Latin grammars became prescriptive, even on oral matters like accent and quantity (Murphy 1974, 149). Grammar thus became more concerned with preserving certain oral qualities, even though this meant imbedding them in a text.

Another example of medieval concern with orality in the *ars poetriae* was the so-called *rithmus,* a technique of composing accented but not metrical verse or prose. Its chief accomplishment was medieval hymnody, but it exercised some influence on the *ars dictaminis* (Murphy 1974, 157–62). The concern of medieval grammarians with *rithmus* actually shows how medieval Latin continued as a living oral speech that gradually forced itself from classical canons and developed a "free verse" and prose style that featured orality. The grammarians' attempt to codify this phenomenon indicates how potent it must have been.

The *ars dictaminis* was a medieval creation, and as such represented a sharp break with ancient rhetorical practice (Murphy 1974, 194ff.). In the ancient world letters were conceived as speeches and were probably dictated to a scribe and read aloud to the recipient by a slave.[7] By 1200 the *rithmus* movement had been refined into what was called *cursus,* a formal sort of rhythmical prose adopted at the Papal Curia, and which compelled scribes actually to count syllables. At roughly the same time, letter writing extended to the legal profession: scribes had to prepare legal documents such as contracts and diplomatic agreements. Consistency had greater value than style for such documents, and treatises on *ars dictaminis* in the thirteenth century began to contain formulas to be copied. *Cursus* and legal writing exercised powerful chirographic constraints on "composition theory"; formulas had a nearly magic power for illiterate rulers of the Middle Ages. By 1300 *ars dictaminis* was nearly totally textualized. For example, Lawrence of Aquilegia's *Practica sive usus dictaminis* (1300) was a collection of formulas for every part of a letter, arranged according to seven different types of audience. The scribe had merely to choose the proper level and then copy out all the appropriate salutations or exordia (Murphy 1974, 258–64).

Preaching is oral performance, but Christian preaching is preaching about writing, that is, scripture. Augustine had dedicated the first three books of his *De doctrina christiana* to showing how the preacher could discover material from his reading of scripture. Medieval preaching manuals tried to provide a short-cut to the material. They began to provide glosses to scripture and to arrange texts in propositions and proofs; they also provided collections of exempla, concordances, lists and charts, and even other sermons, all designed to make it easier for the preacher to find something to say and to have all the necessary material to hand. All such material was put under the rubric of "amplification," that is, the point of the sermon was theoretically expressible in a few sentences, the rest was "amplification." Other manuals also addressed the problem of organization, many giving sample outlines of how the amplified material could be divided and distinguished. In short, the sermon, like the letter, became a genre with a formal structure, and the "art" developed a textualized apparatus to furnish the form with "matter."

The premier form of oral performance in the Middle Ages—and the preeminent form for transmission of formal culture—was the *disputatio*. The disputation's influence upon culture was immense. Although rhetoric may have been relegated to versifying, preaching, and letter writing, logic actually assumed the office of public controversy that rhetoric had held in classical times and late antiquity. Disputation was a kind of adversarial, oral logic, and every teacher and preacher was expected to engage in it (Gilby 1949, 282–96).

The disputants were expected to argue extemporaneously and had to have a great command, not only of formal logic, but also of grammar (for defining and construing the proposition) and of the subject at hand. However, logic supplied the form of the disputation, and medieval logicians applied themselves to developing it with ever-increasing ingenuity and subtlety (Dumitri 1977, II:3–183; Henry 1972). Logic, too, was textualized, developed with a comprehensiveness that far outreached its usefulness for actual debate. Because it seemed useless for actual disputes, late medieval logic acquired a reputation for pedantry and outrageousness that made it the first dog to be kicked whenever humanists got together to discuss the "new learning," the newly recovered texts of the classical rhetoricians.

ORALITY AND WRITING IN RENAISSANCE RHETORIC

Most historians date the Renaissance from the discovery of the complete texts of Quintillian's *Institutio oratoria* in 1417 and Cicero's *De oratore* and *Orator* in 1422. Yet these texts would have meant nothing to the fifteenth century had they not fulfilled a need that preceded their discovery. The fourteenth century had seen the rise of the Italian city-state and a corresponding demand for skills in speaking and writing in the public sphere. Rhetoric became training for the "civil service"; speaking and writing eloquently were the highly prized qualifications for a position in the courts of the city-states. In fourteenth-century Italy, Roman rhetoric was prized as an ideal; Cicero's *doctus orator,* participating in the civil life of the state, was the model for rhetoricians like Salutati, who called rhetoric the path to wisdom (Seigel 1968, 63–98). For him and for the other fourteenth-century humanists, Roman rhetoric and classical Latin were the forces that were to form the true philosopher-orator and, in turn, recreate in the city-states the virtues of the Roman republic. How that ideal changed under political and cultural pressure has been extensively studied by Hans Baron, but the one aspect of the Renaissance that has not been stressed sufficiently is its rediscovery of rhetoric as an oral, performative *disciplina* and its gradual retextualization of rhetoric which, because of the invention of printing, was more thorough and pervasive than in any other preceding age. If rhetoric is an essentially oral art, and if we date the Renaissance from the recovery of interest in rhetoric, then the discovery of the ancient texts may not be the beginning of the Renaissance, but the beginning of its end.

The history of the earliest Renaissance Latin schools has been traced by William Woodward (1904) and Gregor Müller (1969). Those schools used the newly recovered texts of Quintillian and Cicero to replicate the education of the Roman schools. Woodward points out the primacy of orality in the early Renaissance schools of Vittorino da Feltre. Without printed books, each student had to memorize and recite his lesson, thus gradually acquiring mastery over vocabulary and syntax via oral performance (Woodward 1963, 44). Poetry and prose were read aloud to the students, and then every word was defined, the rhythm of the passage was analyzed, its allusions noted, and a moral judgment made about the characters involved. The teaching of rhetoric proper was also orally controlled. Da Feltre insisted that *numerus* (rhythm) was an essential component of rhetorical composition (Woodward 1963, 54). Other rhetorical treatises of the fifteenth century cite the importance of oral performance. Leonardi Bruni Darezzo's *De studiis et literis* (1450) advised the student to practice "reading aloud with clear and exact intonation . . . the music of the prose thus interpreted by the voice will react with advantage upon your own composition, and at the same time will improve your own reading by compelling deliberate and intelligent expression" (Woodward 1963, 125). Aeneas Sylvius Piccolomini's *De liberorum educatione* (1450) gives careful directions for oral delivery (Woodward

1963, 143). Yet even while these early humanists were construing rhetoric as oral performance, the impetus toward textualization was already strong.

The early humanists inherited the full texts of Cicero and Quintillian, and because they found it already textualized, their approach to rhetoric was quite different from that of the Romans they thought they were imitating. The early humanists aimed at teaching style; their program was essentially an imitative one, and what they wanted to imitate was classical Latin. The earliest humanists were, in fact, devoted to the plain style; as Ciceronian rhetoric became more available, it began to predominate as the model of choice. Teaching this style gradually came to depend more on reading, writing, and copying, less on memorization, recitation, and declamation. The commonplace book came to replace the orally trained memory, just as the written *imitatio* came to replace the original declamation. Humanism began, even in the fifteenth century, to transform rhetoric from an orally controlled *disciplina* to a chirographically controlled discipline, but the process accelerated exponentially with the invention of printing. The printing press allowed humanists to textualize rhetoric and to disseminate those texts to a degree unimaginable even a few decades before.

The transformation wrought upon rhetoric by printing is best seen in the career of one man, Desiderius Erasmus, who more than any other humanist saw the potential of printing. Erasmus produced textbooks for the increasingly popular grammar schools, so many books, in fact, that the Dutch printers erected a statue of him. And those books went through hundreds of editions. For example, his *Colloquia,* a set of witty Latin stories and dialogues arranged in ascending degrees of difficulty, were used in schools throughout Europe and America until the twentieth century (Thompson 1965, xxviii). More important was his *Adagia,* a huge collection of quotations and maxims that went through many editions and translations all over Europe. The *Adagia* became a kind of prefabricated commonplace book, supplying hundreds of things to say about everything without burdening the would-be writer with the task of actually reading texts and collecting adages for himself. And it was manifestly for a writer that the *Adagia* were compiled. It is a reference work, not to be interiorized for use in oral performance.

Another work of Erasmus testifies to the shift from orally controlled to chirographically controlled rhetoric. In his *De ratione studii,* he reverses the priorities of Roman pedagogy: "write, write and again write. Supplement writing by learning by heart" (Woodward 1904, 166). The exercises specified in the *De ratione* are similar to those practiced in Rome and advised in Quintillian, yet it is clear that writing has taken precedence over speaking as the mode of instruction (Woodward 1904, 125–31).

Erasmus transformed the teaching of rhetoric by making it textually controlled, but he also changed the theory of rhetoric. This change is apparent in one of Erasmus's most popular works, the *De utraque verborum ac rerum copia,* which went through 150 editions in the sixteenth century.

The *De copia* is Erasmus's *Institutiones oratoriae.* In it he describes how to vary or amplify a speech. *Copia* means *flow* or *facility* of language with a strong military connotation because *copiae* is also the Roman term for *armed forces.* Quintillian in Book X says *copia* cannot be taught because words must flow from the situation or case under consideration. Erasmus, undaunted by this ancient caveat, proceeds to articulate a quasi-systematic way of amplifying any text. The topics were not applied to a case to find suitable arguments, but were used to amplify an argument or subject that already existed in a text. The tropes were used to dilate a text, not to create a forceful argument out of the matter. Erasmus conceived the production of discourse along textual rather than oral lines. His work in rhetoric actually extended the reach of secondary rhetoric and the *De copia* extended *letteraturizzazione* to a general theory of composition, rather than limiting it, as the classical and medieval rhetoricians did, to a particular genre. This extension was impossible without printing, which allowed for the dissemination of such huge compendiums as the *Adagia* as well as other similar commonplace books published by a host of sixteenth-century humanists. Erasmus thought the ancient rhetorical *disciplina* could use the printed book to create the sort of *doctus orator* Quintillian envisioned. In fact, the printed text made the old oral model obsolete even while it was being used to recreate it more efficiently.

During the sixteenth century, the teaching of rhetoric took two diametrically opposed paths: the one in the formation of the Jesuit schools and the other in the pedagogy of Peter Ramus. The first was a formal program that aimed at the humanist goal of uniting learning and religious training and recaptured the Roman synthesis of written and oral pedagogy. The second jettisoned all attempts at religious and moral training and used the printed book as a tool to combine logic and classical rhetoric to form a "method" of logical discourse.

The Jesuit educational ideal is expressed in the famous *Ratio studiorum,* which has been studied by Edward Fitzpatrick (1933); the history of its application has been studied by François de Dainville (1978) and Allen P. Farrell (1938). The *Ratio* was a distillation of the experience of the Jesuit teachers for the first fifty years of the order's history, and it was preeminently a practical guide. It was circulated throughout the Jesuit schools, and it holds up Quintillian, Aristotle, and especially Cicero as its models for rhetoric.

Jesuit pedagogy recaptured many of the characteristics of oral culture that classical rhetoric exhibited. A glance at the daily routine of a Jesuit school shows that students spent more than half the school day either giving or listening to oral performances (Farrell 1938, 346–48). The beginning students started with exercises right out of the progymnasmata, copying fables and maxims (Fitzpatrick 1933, 251–52; Farrell 1938, 276–77). Other exercises for the beginning rhetoric students are straight from Erasmus, for example, descriptions of gardens, churches, paraphrasing verse in prose or vice versa, and accommodating figures of speech to certain subjects (Fitzpatrick 1933, 211). These exercises included recitations of poetry from memory, oral recitations of poetry or prose written by the student (which were corrected orally during the recitation by the teacher), and various contests: contests in declamation, in grammatical analysis, or debates. Finally, there was extemporaneous performance, both by students and teachers (Farrell 1938, 294–95; Fitzpatrick 1933, 251–52). The Jesuits' students did not, however, ignore writing. They kept well-organized commonplace books, copied passages from ancient authors, composed original poetry and prose and, of course, wrote their own plays. But in the early days of the Jesuit schools, until the middle of the seventeenth century, writing was propadeutic to an oral notion of eloquence.

Perhaps the most famous of the Jesuit pedagogical methods was the use of theatrical performances. The Jesuits had their students write and perform plays on classical or religious themes incorporating imitations of poetry and drama. The Jesuit schools thus rediscovered the connection to drama that so permeated Roman rhetoric, and kept their teaching of rhetoric wedded to dramatic performance.

In 1660 Jesuit education entered what de Dainville has called "the crisis of rhetoric" (1978, 195–96). By the end of the seventeenth century Latin grammars used in the French Jesuit schools were being written in French, and the plays in the schools were being performed in French. But it was Ramism that was really the *provocateur* of a change that had ramifications far beyond the borders of Ramus's native France. The *Ratio* had this to say about Ramus: "[The teacher] should beware, however, of imitating Ramus by attaching an exaggerated importance and emphasis to the logical element in Cicero. His speeches should be considered primarily from the rhetorical point of view" (Farrell 1938, 269).

The "exaggerated importance of the logical element in Cicero" is the determining characteristic of Ramism. Its founder, Peter Ramus, made the teaching of the art of persuasive discourse as formalized as the teaching of logic. He conflated Aristotle's treatment of probable argumentation with formal logic to form one "art" of invention and disposition, which he called "judgment" (Ong 1958, 173–96). Ramus called this whole art "dialectic"; rhetoric then became *elocutio* and delivery. This simplification of rhetoric and logic was enormously popular.

It was the printed book that made Ramus's dialectic possible. Ramus contrived to make logic an art of discovery by the process of moving from the general to the particular. Any question or issue could be reduced to a proposition having only two possible answers. The answer chosen could then be restated to yield another dichotomous proposition and so on (Ong 1958, 199–204). Ramus's texts are filled with charts and graphs to illustrate the binomial "method," which is essentially one of visualization. Ideas or propositions continuously generate and link themselves in a spatial field derived from Aristotle's *topoi,* the commonplaces. Ramus took the metaphor of the "place" literally: he envisioned the various *topoi* as fields that generated propositions, but propositions not distinguished, as Aristotle had distinguished them, on the basis of probability or certainty.

Ramism's first result was to divorce thinking from public discourse. The thought process, as Ramus envisioned it, was entirely private: isolate ideas moved and linked in a spatial field. Furthermore, the

linguistic expression of these ideas was assumed to be perfectly unadorned and decontextualized, that is, the idea and its expression were
perfectly matched and independent of any extra-mental context, like
an audience or a situation.

Ramism's second result was to divorce thinking from any figurative
use of language. For Ramus, rhetoric meant decorating logical ideas
with tropes and schemes, a process necessary for gaining a hearing
with the multitude but logically superfluous. The best rhetoric was
no rhetoric. The production of discourse was purely a logical, mental,
and private operation. A corollary, of course, was that any discourse
could be reduced to such a sequence of logical linkage. Hence Ramus's
approach to Cicero against which the *Ratio* warned.

The full impact of Ramism on Western culture may never be understood. Ramus in effect eliminated primary rhetoric and substituted a
kind of secondary logic for secondary rhetoric. He interiorized print
to such an extent that he, in effect, textualized thinking itself, or
claimed to do so. The kind of thinking that writing and reading
inculcates became Ramus's model of rationality itself, and he claimed
to be able to teach it easily and comprehensively.

Ramism's impetus was continued at the school of Port-Royal. There
Claude Lancelot and Antoine Arnauld wrote the *Grammaire générale et
raisonnée de Port-Royal* (1660), and Arnauld and Pierre Nicole published
their *La logique ou l'art de penser* (1662), known as the *Port-Royal Logic*.
Both works went through many editions and were responsible for a
major shift in French education. The *Grammar* studies the "parts of
speech" in logical order and gives rules and examples for their use.
Then it proceeds to explain propositions as grammatical structures
and finally proceeds to "composition": the generating of sustained
discourse by explicating or linking propositions. The *Logic* studies
propositions critically, focusing on how language can accurately reflect things and what conclusions can justifiably be drawn from propositions. It derives rules for detecting false or unjustifiable conclusions
from Descartes' principle of methodic doubt, and celebrates *bon sens,*
a critical faculty applied to propositions according to Descartes' *regula.*

Both the *Grammar* and the *Logic* prescribe a pedagogy that features
writing and nearly excludes oral performance. The grammatical and
logical procedures that the books derive from Cartesian principles
require careful, linear thinking, critical thinking applied to proposi-

tions whose terms are analyzed to determine their *justesse,* their "fit" to reality. There is no consideration of language as historically conditioned, nor is there any consideration given to argument as conditioned by an audience or external circumstances. The Port-Royal texts did away with the *topoi* as sources of argument, but they did not simplify the logical process of thought, and they did maintain the distinction between certain and probable propositions. They share with Ramism a visually controlled model of thought, the divorce of discourse from the public arena, a profound mistrust of figurative language, and the relegation of rhetoric to ornamentation and delivery.

Cartesianism and its pedogogical adaptation at Port-Royal put pressure on the Jesuit schools. Until 1660 the Jesuit schools had held to the original *Ratio,* but after that date it was clear that some kind of modernization of the curriculum was in order. The revision took the form of featuring rules and precepts rather than whole texts. The teaching method became deductive, that is, "methodical." For example, reading, memorizing, reciting, and analyzing sustained texts in a fashion analogous to the old schools of the *grammatici* were replaced by exercises that used short passages to illustrate previously memorized rules. The passages were lifted from context and listed in printed manuals. Second, since Ramus had seized the high ground for dialectic, rhetoric was seen as an art of persuasion rather than as an art of argument and proof. Rhetoric instruction began to taxonomize the tropes and schemes according to their psychological effects. This focus on the passions led to highly formalized delivery. By 1700 *elocutio* had become the first and most important part of rhetoric to be studied in the Jesuit schools (de Dainville 1978, 195). The famed Jesuit academic theater (although most other schools used theatrical productions too) developed into the premier arena for rhetoric conceived as appeals to the passions. The formalization of gesture and voice, along with the focus on the passions, made rhetoric "theatrical" in every sense of the word.

The development of the "new rhetoric" and the Cartesian curriculum of Port-Royal were inconceivable without printed textbooks. For the former, one had to organize the figures of speech according to their psychological potential; to taxonomize texts according to their variety and intensity of passion and to formalize delivery according to predetermined psychological goals requires printing, and not merely as a technical necessity. The latter required disciplined linear thinking and a concept of language as fixed, as if in print. The teaching of rhetoric in seventeenth-century France began with the methods of Renaissance rhetoric, but amplifying texts, adding figures of speech, for example, was useful for training the imagination in oral, especially extemporaneous, performance. It seemed ill-suited for training in writing, however. Once writing had been interiorized, such exercises seemed artificial and flatulent deviations from a "natural" thought progression. The sort of rhetorical exercises described by Peter France in his study of rhetoric in seventeenth- and eighteenth-century France (1972) were fated to fall into disrepute. Enlightenment thinkers were unanimous in their condemnation of rhetoric, a rhetoric already confined to the arousal of passions by spurious means. The discarnate mind operating with fixed meanings replaced the rhetorically trained imagination as the model of reason.

French discourse in the seventeenth century became "discursive." Descartes wrote discourses and meditations: forms that were supposedly modeled on conversation rather than formal oratorical speech. Later Diderot reclaimed the literary dialogue as a vehicle for serious literature. But these oral forms were themselves the product of "literate" speech, the speech of people who had interiorized writing. The speech that characterized *civilité* in the salons contrasted sharply with the adversativeness of the old rhetorical world.

With the Enlightenment we arrive at that time when Vico began his career. The culture of Europe was being decisively shaped by the culture, the *civilisation,* of France. But Vico lived in a milieu different from that of the French, a milieu more oral than seventeenth-century France and one that preserved a good part of the humanist tradition. To see how this oral milieu permeated Vico's Naples and its baroque culture is the next task.

2 Oral Arenas in Vico's Naples

In Vico's Naples contradictions and oppositions lived in constant dynamic balance. Unlike Venice, Naples had no continuous, consistent form of government; unlike Florence, Naples had neither Republican tradition nor the wherewithal to create one.[1] What it did have was a sediment formed by a sequence of different political, social, and legal formations, each superimposed on the other but not displacing or even controlling its predecessors.[2] The Spanish, who ruled Naples in Vico's time, repeatedly attempted to impose their own system on the city and to bring its traditional social forces to heel. At the same time, the new philosophy of the Enlightenment was reaching Naples and being discussed in salons and informally organized groups of intellectuals. These discussions were not merely speculative, for Naples was the scene of a confrontation between Enlightenment philosophy and social practice.

The University of Naples and the law courts were the two focuses of that practice, and these two institutions formed the immediate context of Vico's rhetorical theory. Intense orality characterized these two institutions. The university and the law courts continued to feature oral performance and adversarial thinking in ways that decisively shaped their practices—and their supporting theories. Because they were the arenas of social conflict, the university and the courts were also the focal points of reform, and reformers competed for their control. Before describing the competition that was the matrix of Vico's thought, a brief account of how Neapolitan society came to be so complex is in order.

Southern Italy was civilized even before the founding of Rome. It was *Magna Graecia,* the site of extensive Greek colonies and the birthplace of Pythagoras and Pythagoreanism. After incorporation (but not acculturation) into the Roman empire, it remained the playground of wealthy Romans. Tiberius had a favorite villa on Capri, and nearby Pompeii and Herculaneum were prosperous, light-hearted urban centers until Mount Vesuvius destroyed them in A.D. 79. In late antiquity and the early middle ages, southern Italy saw the growth of independent communes composed of small landholders. In the eleventh century, southern Italy and Sicily were conquered by the Normans and eventually ruled by the Emperor Frederick II, the *stupor mundi,* whose intellectual curiosity and forceful personality astonished his contemporaries. He brought southern Italy to considerable prominence and is the ruler whom Jacob Burckhardt credits with raising the state to the level of a work of art (1960, 40–43). Early in the thirteenth century, the Kingdom of Naples became part of the Angevin possessions, but shortly thereafter Naples and Sicily became two separate kingdoms. More important, in 1282, the feudal barons, descended from the Normans, increased their independence to an extent that made safeguards against abuse of their power negligible even by medieval standards (Gleijeses 1977, 315–31). Thus a potent form of feudalism came to southern Italy against a background of imperial conquest.

Naples remained under Angevin rule until 1443 when Alfonso of Aragon became king of Naples through marriage to a surviving Angevin queen. The Aragonese dynasty brought Spanish culture and tradition to Naples–another layer in the sediment of Neapolitan life. Aragonese monarchs granted the populace many economic rights and thus freed them from the heavy hand of local barons. Furthermore, the Aragonese were influenced by Florentine humanism and brought its culture to Naples.

The political result of royal concessions and humanistic culture was to make Naples a Renaissance city-state rather than a feudal kingdom. The king came to be seen as the center of national identity and as a refuge against abuses of baronial power. This feeling survived even after World War II, when southern Italy voted decisively for a restoration of the monarchy and against a democratic government.

Aragonese rule lasted until the end of the fifteenth century. In 1503 Naples became a Spanish vice-regency, and in 1529 Charles V annexed Naples to his vast empire. The Spanish viceroys set out to reduce the power of the barons still more and to implement Spanish royal power in the Kingdom of Naples. What occurred was typically Neapolitan: the barons became strong supporters of the Spanish administration and tried to bargain with it to retain or enhance their ancestral privileges. On the other hand, the local communes both bargained with the barons and looked to the royal administration for continued or restored economic independence.[3] Hence, the Spanish administration came to mediate between nobility and commoners, and, as we shall see, the situation made lawyers a new civil class.

With Spanish rule came increased political and social power for the Catholic Church. Unlike the reign of Frederick II, whose contempt for the Church has become a historical commonplace, Spanish rule saw continuing growth in the power and prestige of the Church, and especially of ecclesiastical courts. The Inquisition was introduced at Naples in 1564 and proceeded to function intermittently while subject to popular harassment (Gleijeses 1977, 580–81 and passim). Thus another layer of political power and culture was laid to form Neapolitan life.

Feudal law, ecclesiastical law, Spanish law and administration, ancient traditions of common law, and the inheritance of Renaissance humanism formed fluid forces, constantly acting and reacting against each other in social practice and providing endless stimulation and entertainment for theoreticians. Those theoreticians focused on the law and the university because that was where the Spanish administration focused its efforts at reform, and those two institutions were the scene of Vico's career.

The university was founded by Frederick II in the twelfth century. During the Renaissance the university added chairs of eloquence— one of which Vico held—and allowed the study of formal logic to decline. The curriculum and organization of the university, as Vico knew it, had been established in 1616 by the Viceroy Count Lemnos in his *De regimine studiorum,* otherwise known as the *Prammatica di Lemnos* (Torraca 1924, 270). The *Prammatica* stipulated the methods for conducting classes, the procedures for examination and for selecting professors, as well as the organization of the faculty. The *Prammatica*'s prescriptions reveal the pervasive influence of orally controlled rhetoric, and orality in general, within the university.

The *Prammatica* established the lecture method as the format for all classes, and the regulations governing the lectures reveal how seriously they were taken. For example, students were fined for missing lectures or for being tardy. On the other hand, the tardiness of professors was also noted scrupulously by the university administration (Torraca 1924, 390). But most of the regulations attempt to enforce good order, and especially silence, in the lecture hall. A whole catalog of noises is specifically forbidden: talking, whistling, wheezing, groaning, and shouting (Torraca 1924, 394). The *Prammatica* was designed to control student violence, which was rampant in the sixteenth and early seventeenth centuries (Torraca 1924, 377–78). For example, before the *Prammatica,* in 1557, a regulation appears in the university records prohibiting students from bringing weapons to class. In 1558 another regulation appears, this one prohibiting students from being accompanied to class by *servants* carrying weapons (Torraca 1924, 377).

The *Prammatica* illustrates Walter Ong's contention that orally controlled education tends to be adversative, that is, that it conceives truth as emerging from a conflict conducted according to rules that both sublimate physical aggression and provide a sort of ritual initiation into adult society for those who survive the contest (Ong 1981). The *Prammatica* attempted to provide such rules, and they show how oral performance was the mode by which truth was structured and aggression channeled.

Students graduated only after an oral examination, and it was a manifestly adversative procedure. The candidate was examined by a panel of teachers before an audience of his fellow students. If he passed, he was praised in a set speech recorded in the *Prammatica.* The candidate is compared to that noble Roman who stretched his hand into flames to prove his trustworthiness and courage, but the candidate "placed not only his hand but his whole body into the fire by his labor and sleepless nights *[vigilatem]*" (Torraca 1924, 403). The speech evokes both *virtù* and Roman *pietas.*

The competitiveness of oral rhetoric is even more apparent in the procedures for selecting new faculty. Vico himself participated in such a competition for a chair of jurisprudence, and he recorded the event in his *Autobiography.* Vico's account of his examination corresponds with the procedure outlined in the *Prammatica.* The candidates for a chair were to present lectures before a panel of faculty members. On the day before the lectures they were to choose their subjects by drawing lots. Then they would have twenty-four hours to prepare their presentations. On the following day at nine o'clock they would commence to lecture by turns in the university theater. When the lectures were finished, the contestants *(oppositori)* were to be seated and respond to questions and challenges from the faculty panel (Torraca 1924, 291–92). The procedure is calculated to test ad hoc verbal performance, especially the *copia* of the contestants.

Vico describes how he had twenty-four hours to prepare a two-hour speech commenting on a passage from Justinian's *Pandects*. He records how he made copious notes, reduced them to a single page, and then spoke with "such a copiousness of expression as might have served another two hours' harangue" *(Autobiography* 163). Vico also describes how he ingeniously recovered from a slip of the tongue during his lecture: "Once only, because of the difficulty of the word *progegrammenōn,* he hesitated for a moment, but then continued: 'It is no wonder that I was brought to a halt, for the very *antitupia* [harshness] of the word put me off.' Many thought he had allowed himself to seem confused only in order to recompose himself with so apt and elegant a Hellenism" (163).

This sort of impromptu speaking, displaying erudition and quick intelligence, was the mainstay of the university program. Vico concludes his account of the contest by reporting that he copied his speech in writing the next day and distributed copies to his friends. Nevertheless, he lost the competition to a charlatan, a notorious seducer of servant girls whose one attempt at publication had to be withdrawn after being exposed as plagiarism *(Autobiography* 10).

Erudition and extemporaneous speaking were the qualities desired in university professors, and the use of extemporaneous performance for examinations and competitions meant that they shared a pedagogical method despite the differences in subject matter. In fact, the faculties were far more diverse than they are in modern universities. Vico's faculty at the university would have included not only eloquence but also logic, ethics, metaphysics, mathematics, law, and medicine. The faculties did not have today's disciplinary boundaries; on the contrary, they were unified by a common rhetorical praxis. They all aimed at knowledge conceived as *copia* displayed in oral performance.

In 1703 the government tried to institute a modern academic organization, complete with disciplines and departments, at the University of Naples, and that transformation was one of the most important events in Vico's intellectual career (Torraca 1924, 270). The reform of 1703 was one of the few attempts that eventually succeeded in changing the University of Naples, although it was nearly forty years before the reform went into full effect. Eight faculties were created out of the existing faculty, faculties formed on disciplinary lines familiar today. The reforms were not permanent; in 1707 Naples was occupied by Austria, and the university was returned to its traditional organization. But in 1732 another reorganization of the faculty was proposed by the royal Chaplain, who had responsibility for the university. This reform proposed eliminating three of the six chairs in law. Instead of these chairs, there would be a chair of "natural law" and another chair of *"jus regni."* A chair of ethics would be abolished because that subject would become the purview of the chair of natural law (Amodeo 1902, 5–7). It was between 1703 and 1732, when the university was vacillating between tradition and reform, that Vico produced his most significant work.

The proposed reforms indicate the influence of Cartesianism on the university. The reforms of 1703 substituted a disciplinary rationale for the rhetorical methodology that had united the faculty. The reforms of 1732 shifted away from Roman law to a rationalistic view of law that separated *jus* from law, and in fact put *jus* within the purview of the monarchy. These reforms were not enacted until 1735, and then in modified form. Two chairs of law were eliminated, and the chair of *jus regni* founded, but the chair of natural law never was. The final shift to the disciplinary organization occurred in 1742, when chairs were founded in botany, chemistry, anatomy, experimental physics, astronomy, church history, Hebrew, and municipal law (Torraca 1924, 450–51). The hegemony of experimental science and scientific method was firmly established. Vico resigned his chair of eloquence. It passed on to his son for a few years, but the position was never filled again.

The struggle by which rationalistic and scientific method replaced rhetoric in the university curriculum was a long one. Vico played a role in that struggle, but there is no agreement about the extent of his influence.[4] Nonetheless, some facts are known.

The center of Cartesianism was the *Academia degli Investiganti,* a kind of Neapolitan salon that met to discuss the new philosophy and the new science making such an impact in France.[5] The *Investiganti* studied the metaphysical implications of Cartesianism and empiricism and were preoccupied with atomism as a possible way of maintaining a link between the physical and material realms (Badaloni 1961, 79–126). Of course, these discussions had an impact on the university and generated controversies about the proper methodology and subject matter for university education. The foremost defender of Cartesian method was Leonardo di Capua, one of the founders of the *Investiganti* (Jacobelli 1960, 61). His foremost opponent was Domenico Aulisio, who resisted Cartesian method but tried to find a third way between the ancients versus moderns' quarrel (Di Giovanni, *Il "De nostri,"* 147). Aulisio wanted to mediate between a dogmatic traditionalism that maintained that knowledge was located in ancient texts and Cartesian epistemology, which held that truth was deducible from simple premises. During their polemics Aulisio praised Vico's *De nostri temporis studiorum ratione* for its pedagogy, which seemed to offer a defense of traditional humanism that did not totally exclude Cartesian critical method from some role in university education (Di Giovanni, *Il "De nostri,"* 147). Vico ultimately rejected Descartes' claim to exclusive validity in method and retained the humanistic view that rhetorical education provided a better basis for participation in political and community life.

Various other groups or salons addressed these and similar problems. One was the group of intellectuals who gathered about Giuseppe Valletta. More important, the Valletta group found a colleague who may have influenced Vico's idea of *sensus communis:* Anthony Ashley Cooper, the third Earl of Shaftesbury.[6] Shaftesbury visited Naples in his youth and returned there to spend his last days before dying of asthma in 1713. By the time of his death Shaftesbury's *Characteristicks* may have been known in Naples, including his essay on *Sensus Communis: An Essay on the Freedom of Wit and Humour* (Croce 1923, 9). Furthermore, Vico is reputed to have visited Shaftesbury at his palazzo and to have frequented the Valletta circle (Croce 1923, 8). Hence, Shaftesbury's writings on *sensus communis* bear some looking into because of the possibility of historical influence, both positive and negative.

Shaftesbury's *Sensus Communis: An Essay on the Freedom of Wit and Humour* was published in 1709 and included in the 1711 edition of the *Characteristicks*. It proposes irony as the test of truth, that is, its theme is the use of irony as a way of legitimating truth claims. The ability to engage in, and receive, raillery and ridicule is Shaftesbury's test of "good humour," the moral sense that gives evidence that its possessor is moral himself. *Sensus communis* is what makes irony possible; it is the sense to which irony appeals and in juxtaposition to which irony is recognized. In describing how this sense comes to exist, Shaftesbury explicates a theory of culture and education that differs from Vico's, but within which can be seen the agenda Vico had set for himself.

Shaftesbury explicitly relates *sensus communis* to moral sentiment, the philosophical concept for which he is best known: "A publick Spirit can come only from a social Feeling or *Sense of Partnership* with Human Kind. Now there are none so far from being *Partners* in this *Sense,* or sharers in this *common Affection,* as they who scarcely know *an Equal,* nor consider themselves as subject to any law of *Fellowship* or *Community.* And thus Morality and good Government go together" (1:06).

Shaftesbury tries to establish the source of this public feeling in individual private feeling. Thus he is led to account for the beginning of human society, and he does it in a way that is far different from the way Vico will describe it in the *New Science.* But Shaftesbury's account of social origins is consistent with his own principles and became popular with later writers like Rousseau. Shaftesbury has the first humans forming tribes and clans out of a sense of natural affection. Then the tribes notice "a Necessity for continuing this good Correspondence and Union, that to have no *Sense* or Feeling of this kind, no Love of *Country, Community,* or anything *in common,* would be the same as to be insensible even of the plainest Means of *Self-preservation,* and most necessary condition of *Self-Enjoyment*" (I:111). Shaftesbury here posits that *sensus communis* is a natural affection that has become self-conscious. The clans and tribes realize that their fellow feeling is itself a good thing, and thus they have a desire or feeling for it. Thus the community experiences what is the commonplace definition of Shaftesbury's moral sentiment: a feeling for a feeling, that is, a desire, a feeling, for the feeling of community.

Shaftesbury continues by claiming that, whereas tribes and clans may form themselves out of a natural affection, larger units, like nations or states, form themselves, not from the sensible affection, but "in Idea: according to that general view or Notion of a *State* or *Commonwealth*" (I:112). In other words, the larger units of society depend upon the idea of the feeling of *sensus communis* rather than the feeling itself.

After discussing how *sensus communis* manifests itself in social units, Shaftesbury considers its manifestation in the individual. First he describes it negatively; the opposite of *sensus communis* is the spirit of faction, which is the "Abuse or Irregularity of that *Social Love,* and *common* Affection, which is natural to Mankind" (I:114). Individuals who possess *sensus communis* are the least likely to join parties. "They are secure of their Temper; and possess themselves too well, to be in danger of entring to warmly into any cause, or engaging deeply with any Side or Faction" (I:115). Here one sees the relation of Shaftesbury's *sensus communis* to irony. *Sensus communis* is an idea of fellow feeling that inhibits partisanship and promotes detachment and cool judgment. But how does one come to possess this quality?

Shaftesbury's description of the positive qualities of an individual who possesses *sensus communis* indicates a serious problem in his account. First, he says that "A man of thorow *Good Breeding,* whatever else he be, is incapable of doing a rude or brutal Action. He never *deliberates* in this case, or considers of the matter by prudential Rules or Self-Interest and Advantage. He acts from his Nature, in a manner necessarily, and without Reflection: and if he did not, it were impossible for him to answer his Character, or be found that truly well-bred Man, on every occasion" (I:129–30). Thus the man with *sensus communis* is a man of "good breeding" for whom virtuous action is "natural," that is, unreflective. He does not need to think about behaving well, he just does it. The individual, presumably, has been bred into natural behavior.

Shaftesbury then turns from his "man of good breeding" to a man of no breeding, the "common honest man" whom, he says, "whilst left to himself, and undisturbed by Philosophy and subtle Reasonings about his Interest gives no other answer to the Thought of Villany, than that *he can't possibly find in his heart* to set about it, or conquer the natural Aversion he has to it. And this is *natural,* and *just*" (I:132). Here *sensus communis* is predicated of the "common" man. One is left in doubt as to the relation of breeding or education to the sort of natural behavior Shaftesbury describes. Is *sensus communis* natural, or is it the result of education? If it is the result of education, then of what sort of education? Shaftesbury does not resolve the first issue; rather he maintains the tension between education and nature. On the second issue, he is more direct. The education involved is aesthetic, an education in taste.

Shaftesbury describes the possessors of *sensus communis* as "gentlemen of fashion," whom he describes as "those to whom a natural good genius, or the force of a good education, has given a sense of what is naturally graceful and becoming" (I:89). *Sensus communis* is a sense of what is "naturally graceful and becoming," which itself may or may not come naturally to its possessor. Shaftesbury here is proposing the paradox that people may have to be educated into naturalness. Rather than resolving this ambivalence, he simply admits it. But it does not rest easy within his theory. Rather, it is undermined by the double meaning of "fashion" in "gentlemen of fashion." The phrase can mean gentlemen who are au courant in styles of speech, dress, and art, and it can mean gentlemen who have been fashioned, that is, men who have been groomed and trained to behave according to certain preexisting models or rules. "Fashion" in either case implies certain standards with which one's behavior and appearance are congruous, and Shaftesbury maintains that the congruity can be either "natural" or learned, but those to whom it is natural are no longer considered "common honest men," but rather men who have a "natural good genius," a rather uncommon commodity.

The contradiction between learned or natural *sensus communis* really cannot be resolved in terms of "fashion" or "genius." Shaftesbury moves the issue to the sphere of ethics. How does the possessor of *sensus communis* behave in the face of ethical conflict? This tack leads Shaftesbury to reconcile the contradiction in terms of aesthetically formed behavior rather than by a stipulative definition of *sensus communis*.

Some by mere Nature, others by Art and practice, are Masters of an Ear in Musick, an Eye in Painting, a Fancy in the Ordinary things of Ornament and Grace, a Judgment in Proportions of all kinds, and a general good Taste in most of those Subjects which make the Amusements and Delight of the ingenious People of the World. Let such Gentlemen as these be as extravagant as they please, or as irregular in their Morals; they must at the same time discover their

Inconsistency, live at variance with themselves, and in contradiction to that Principle, on which they ground their highest Pleasure and Entertainment. (I:135)

Shaftesbury argues here that the principle of Taste, which regulates choice of pleasure, must also regulate conduct, and if it does not, then the individual is confronted with a self-contradiction: the objects of pleasure are pleasant because of certain principles that behavior violates. In short, pleasures are not pleasant because conduct is not "pleasing."

The principle of Taste is closely related to *sensus communis* because Taste can be either learned or natural, but it must be communal, that is, it is formed and judged with an eye on social behavior and mores; eccentric Taste is a contradiction in terms. Second, Taste is harmonic, essentially a proportion of parts, a harmony of design, whether it be in a musical piece, a painting, or a well-ordered life. The principles of harmony can be learned or, in some gifted persons, they can be innate. But they are principles that are rational, and which are shared by a community of fashion. Thus *sensus communis* is that principle of taste, founded in harmony and reason, shared by gentlemen of fashion and which provides clear guidance to aesthetic judgment and ethical choices. *Sensus communis* is, then, a rational standard according to which questions of taste and self-interest can be judged, and are judged, with spontaneous clarity. Shaftesbury concludes his account of *sensus communis* with an account of its behavioral origins in the individual.

True Interest is wholly on *one* side, or *the other*. All between is Inconsistency, Irresolution, Remorse, Vexation, and an Ague-Fit: from hot to cold; from one Passion to another quite contrary; a perpetual Discord of Life; and an alternate Disquiet and Self-dislike. The only Rest or Repose must be thro *one, determin'd, considerate Resolution: which when once taken, must be courageously kept; and the Passions and Affections brought under obedience to it; the Temper steel'd and harden'd to the Mind; the Disposition to the Judgment. Both must agree; else all must be Disturbance and Confusion. So that to think with one's self in good earnest, "Why may not one do this *little* Villany, or commit this *one* Treachery, and but for *once,"* is the most ridiculous Imagination in the world, and contrary to COMMON SENSE. (I:131–32)

Shaftesbury here locates *sensus communis* in the will. Whatever the impact of education, fashion, or genius, the moral force of *sensus communis* derives from an individual act of will, a resolution to follow "good taste" as an ideal, as a feeling worth feeling even when one does not feel it, and to regulate one's conduct by it. This means making the shared standards of good conduct one's own and embracing the fellow feeling on which they, and the pleasures of human society, are grounded. Shaftesbury ultimately resolves the nature versus education polarity in volition.

Shaftesbury's idea of *sensus communis* has several similarities to Vico's, as we shall see, but it also has some essential differences. Shaftesbury sees a connection between ethical behavior and aesthetic judgment. His idea of Taste attempts to make that connection explicit by founding both ethics and pleasure in a sense of harmony and proportion available to reason and shared by those who have learned it, or who possess it as a form of "natural genius." Where Shaftesbury differs from Vico is in the source of *sensus communis*. Shaftesbury places it in the will informed by an ideal of Taste perceived and held as the "common sense" of the best part of society. Vico addresses the larger issue of where *sensus communis* is to be found *in the community.* Vico eventually sought the source of *sensus communis,* and he found it not in a "natural affection," but in myth. But that occurs in the *New Science.* At the time Shaftesbury was in Naples Vico was working on the problem of *sensus communis* as a legal concept grounded in rhetorical education.

Vico took it for granted that education was supposed to prepare one for participation in public life, and he felt the best preparation was, first, rhetoric and, second, the law. However the law was also being subjected to repeated attempts at reform, attempts also inspired by Cartesian philosophy. The university reform that separated *jus regni* from natural law, and then limited ethics to the latter, parallels developments in Neapolitan legal reform. Along with the conflict over the university curriculum, the conflict over the reform of the Neapolitan court system and its laws in general formed the other immediate context of Vico's thought.

In Vico's time the legal system of Naples was perhaps more chaotic than any other aspect of the city's life.[7] Neapolitan law included, first, common law developed throughout the Middle Ages and the Renaissance among the communities of private, non-noble landowners and townspeople. Next was feudal law and its system of privileges and duties regulating the relations of nobles and commoners. Third, was the legal system imported with the Spanish vice-regency with its absolutist principles. Finally, there was ecclesiastical law and its agent, the Inquisition, whose jurisdiction included not only religious but also much we now consider civil matters such as marriage law and rights of clergy. These various legal systems and their judicial and enforcement agencies had no distinct boundaries. On the contrary, their claims to jurisdiction overlapped, and their agencies frequently competed.

The chaos of the system was due primarily to one historical fact: until 1806 Naples had no written code of laws. The "law" was, in fact, a set of precedents, customs, usages, that existed primarily in oral form, and some written decrees and proclamations. Even the written decrees and proclamations were subjected to intensive interpretation in the light of tradition.

In Naples law meant arguing from precedents that were not written down, but that were preserved in oral tradition. Thus the legal system shared the inheritance of oral rhetoric with the university. But the practice of law in Naples had little to do with the Roman law that formed the content of university courses. Lectures in Justinian's *Pandects,* for example, were singularly unsuited for actual legal practice in Naples. Law students studied a body of law that Naples did not have, but which was the one body of law that epitomized legal thought— Roman law. To this extent law students exercised themselves in an ideal realm. But legal education did do one thing for its students: it gave them experience in legal argument, in forensic rhetoric, and that was certainly a sine qua non for legal practice in Vico's Naples.

The role of lawyers (or *togati)* and of the law has been investigated by Raffael Ajello and Pierluigi Rovito, and their findings illuminate the role rhetoric played in Vico's Naples. The *togati* actually fulfilled a dual role in Neapolitan society: that of courtroom pleaders and that of private consultants or negotiators. For both roles the *togati* needed great skill in extemporaneous oral performance.

In criminal cases the *togati* were called upon to perform in the most dramatic circumstances. Criminal cases were tried very quickly after an arrest was made, frequently on the same day. The defense lawyer may have had only a few hours at most to prepare. Under such circumstances, he had to marshal his case from legal precedent, from an analysis of the facts and from whatever extenuating circumstances existed. From these materials he had to make a forceful plea, well organized and emotionally compelling.

Of course, all legal pleading was done in Latin. The use of Latin had two effects on the practice of the law. First, it made the whole legal system a specialized discipline inaccessible to the ordinary citizen. The second effect of Latin was to connect legal pleading to the tradition of humanist rhetoric, especially to the tradition of Roman forensic rhetoric. Thus, even though Roman law was not applicable to Neapolitan society, Roman legal oratory was obviously the model for the practice of law, and with it the whole tradition of Latin literature that supported Roman and humanistic rhetorical training. These two effects combined to produce a legal praxis both more flexible and more performative than modern law.

The practice of law in Vico's Naples featured jurisprudence to a far greater degree than in societies with written legal codes. Jurisprudence, roughly defined, means adapting the law to a specific case, judging to what extent the case fits the law and how extenuating circumstances affect the law's application. Such judgments include an interpretation of the literal meaning of statutory law as opposed to, or qualified by, its effect in a particular case in the light of its intent. In Neapolitan society, where no codex existed, jurisprudence meant balancing conflicts of interest, and not only conflicts of interest, but also conflicts of jurisdiction, in the light of a complex of legal custom, oral tradition, and disorganized and conflicting legal documents. Such jurisprudence had to occur within oral pleading based on oral tradition. Forensic rhetoric provided the form for such pleading. Professor Biagio Di Giovanni refers to the legal system as "the culture of jurisdictionalism" *(la cultura di giurisdizionalismo)* *("Scienza e vita civile"* 432). In some respects rhetorically controlled jurisprudence *was* the practice of law; it played the same role in Naples' orally controlled legal system that construal of statute law plays in our own legal system. In such a culture an attorney would proceed according to methods far different from those associated with twentieth-century legal practice.

First, the lawyer would have to apply rhetorical *inventio* to a body of traditional law that did not exist in any easily accessible form. Hence the *topoi* would be invaluable in developing a case. Second, since there was no codex to focus the case, the pleader would be free to organize the material in a more ad hoc fashion. Such a performance would place a premium on using figurative language to focus argument and emotion, drawing on the oral tradition of the law and bringing it to bear on the case. Finally, although Roman law played no practical role in the adjudication, the attorney could marshall all the forces of Roman literature, the inheritance of humanism, and bring them to bear on the case. All in all, Neapolitan legal praxis required primary rhetoric, ad hoc extemporaneous performance, and was even more relentlessly oral in that its subject matter, Neapolitan law, existed in traditional, oral form rather than in organized codified form.

Descriptions of Neapolitan law courts confirm that the practice of law was essentially oral. The courts were well known for their pomp and ceremony. Ajello has pointed out that the *togati* considered themselves to be practicing a kind of "rhetorical heroism" elevated beyond the concerns of ordinary life. The law was a secret discipline learned only through long apprenticeship and frequently compared to the vocation of arms (Ajello 1980, 19–20). Various legal officers and judges each had their own appropriate costume. The proceedings were carried on with prescribed rituals. In fact, the courts were so "dramatic" that they were a tourist attraction. One contemporary observer reports with amazement that a visiting German prince stayed in Naples for eight days without once visiting the courts to witness the "chaos" there (Galasso 1971, 21).

The second role of the *togati* was that of go-between, of consultant or negotiator in business, political affairs, and civil actions. Parties in civil suits had a real interest in avoiding litigation because civil actions, unlike criminal cases, could drag on for years, providing pain to the litigants and diversion to spectators. Croce cites the amazement of visitors to Naples at the intense interest in even the most hair-splitting legal questions (1971, 141). Instead of rapid oral performance, the premium in these cases was on thorough, philological analysis of all existing cases, precedents, and any other written material. Marshaling this data, without a codified law, then interpreting it according to the arcane principles of etymology and legal theory, could take decades.

Rather then submit to this, litigants frequently called upon their attorneys to negotiate a settlement out of court, but such negotiations were rather different from those of our own legal practice. When equipped with a written code, lawyers can negotiate on the principle of probable settlement. As Justice Holmes remarked, a lawyer's job is to predict what the courts will do. But in Naples such predictions could not be based on existing codes, so negotiators had more room to argue about what could or could not be justified. They could appeal to the oral tradition and to legal practice. Hence some sense of what the community feels to be right would have to play a central role in such negotiations as it would in court pleading itself.

The Neapolitan judicial system was an arena in which the various classes and interests of the society competed in a kind of ritual combat. The *togati* served as a kind of legal *condottieri* available to serve barons, communes, or the government. They considered themselves the heroes of this perpetual civic struggle. The *togati* needed a reputation for disinterestedness as much as a reputation for skill in verbal combat and so could not afford to join any side or class if they wished to continue their careers.

While it may have afforded them endless hours of entertainment and spectacle, the Neapolitan legal system did not please many legal theoreticians, nor did it please the Spanish vice-regal administration. Simply put, the system prevented the government from using the law as an administrative tool. The system favored the status quo and made any sort of social reform difficult to achieve. Oral tradition is always resistant to change simply because tradition is so difficult to retain. Traditional societies are too preoccupied with conserving tradition to attempt changing it consciously. But the *togati* themselves had an interest in reform. They had replaced the feudal barons as the administrative class under the Spanish. The law courts, with their potential for endless maneuver and delay, seriously impeded the Spanish administration. Thus, the administration sponsored many attempts at codifying the laws or reforming the legal system, and several Neapolitan philosophers and legal thinkers dedicated themselves to eliminating its many abuses.[8]

The debate over legal reform fueled the theoretical studies that formed the immediate background of Vico's notion of *sensus communis* and its relation to orally controlled rhetoric. Reformers like Francesco D'Andrea turned to Cartesian philosophy as a new basis for law, while the defenders of the status quo had to find a philosophical basis for their position that could stand up to the epistemological challenge Cartesianism implied. The immediate goal of the reformers was, of course, a written codex. But to produce one would imply reconciling the conflicts within the oral tradition and case law. Furthermore, it would imply clarifying jurisdictional claims. These issues could not be settled merely by writing down the laws. Attempts to codify Neapolitan law were continually frustrated (Rovito 1981, 401–54). By 1737, the issue became further complicated by competing editions of the laws (Ajello 1976, 97). The issue rapidly became "what were the laws" and, ultimately, "what was law." Neapolitan legal theory, among which Vico's works must be listed, was developed out of this very practical problem.

D'Andrea, the chief of these reformers, was a gifted lawyer and courtroom pleader,[9] who supported the Cartesian-inspired reforms in the university and wrote two polemics defending Leonardo D'Capua, their originator. He was also an accomplished scholar and brought philology to bear on legal problems. The example of D'Andrea's pleading had a profound effect on Neapolitan legal practice, but he did not produce any theoretical works of his own. Rather, other theoreticians derived their ideas from his practice.

The Cartesian reformers sought to eliminate the very basis of Neapolitan law: the doctrine of *communis opinio,* or *consensus gentium,* which Aristotle cited in his *Organon* as providing the grounds for probable truth in cases that admitted no demonstrative conclusion. Here was the heart of the Neapolitan system as Vico knew it. *Communis opinio* provided the link among customary law, legal tradition, and rhetoric conceived as dealing with probability. Cartesian reformers invoked Descartes' critique of *communis opinio* in the *Discourse on Method.* They pointed out that *communis opinio* assumed that reason was authoritative, that the rational could be known by its manifestation in historically valid authority. But they then argued, along with Descartes, that experience had shown that this notion was insufficient and that reason was in fact the *ratio* of the individual. Ajello describes the effect of this critique:

The negation of the *consensus gentium* as the source of truth, performed by Descartes and then by Hobbes, by Spinoza, by Pufendorf,
by Bayle, by Locke, radically invalidated that constitutional *fictio* on
which was founded the common law, and finally, to a certain extent,
all the constituted order. If the marvellous consensus of all educated
people had confirmed the absolute value of the *Ordo* [established
order] elaborated from its foundations in Roman law in late medieval
and humanistic judicial science, then to deny the significance of the
consensus signified denying the same foundations of the *respubblica*
and implied trusting to a reason of state implicitly free of every rule
of law and finally susceptible of being overshadowed by tyranny, a
prospect which had not particularly preoccupied Cola Capasso, but
which neither Gravina, nor Doria, nor Vico was able to accept
without reserve. (1976, 172–73)[10]

By substituting Cartesian rationality for *consensus* the reformers
were able to shift the whole basis of legal theory from tradition to the
present. Cartesian theory offered a justification for innovative social
change achieved through the courts and administration, an ability to
adapt the law to changing social conditions by making the basis for
legislation "rational" rather than "traditional." Of course, this raises
the issue of authority: who decides what is rational? The answer
was, of course, the royal administration. The administration was
dominated by bureaucrats trained in Cartesian method, including
many *togati* who practiced what Ajello has called "rhetorical Cartesianism," that is, they argued law cases and generally operated according
to the canons of Cartesian logic with its focus on certitude rather than
Aristotelian logic and its admission of probability into the realm of
practical affairs (1980, 109). These *togati* saw Cartesian method as the
best way of achieving the social ends of the administration.

The Spanish administration was reaching to Cartesianism to put its
absolutist ambitions on a philosophical basis that could rival, and defeat,
the philosophical ground of Neapolitan legal "chaos." The administration, in short, was claiming to define reason and to define it as its own
possession. There is no doubt that Neapolitan life needed serious social
reform, but whether that reform could be achieved by an absolutist regime, and a foreign one at that, was another issue, and whether
the price of that reform might not be too high was also an issue.

Against the Cartesian reformers were arrayed the forces of the traditional establishment. But it would be a mistake to construe the conflict as one between modern reformers and entrenched traditionalists. On the contrary, by the second decade of the eighteenth century, the Cartesians dominated the administration and the *togati*. They were in the majority and held all the advantages of being the avant-garde as well. Their opponents were on the defensive, and the defense centered around finding an epistemological basis for traditional law that could rival the claims of Cartesian rationalism.

The problem that faced Vico and the other defenders of Neapolitan legal practice was finding a way to unite common law with natural law, that is, showing how the traditional, customary law of the kingdom could be grounded in a *jus naturalis,* a given "natural" order that in turn was available to reason. This was not an easy task; the only body of law that could support such a claim was Roman law. Roman law could be interpreted, analyzed, and investigated to reveal some sort of coherence between legal theory and natural reason. But Neapolitan law, or medieval law for that matter, was too diffuse to yield such insight. Futhermore, the defenders were faced with the additional problem of access: Cartesian *raison* was available to anyone, but who could know the natural law, and how? As Ajello's statement, cited previously, implies, the *consensus gentium* was really a *consensus* of the learned who had access to the Roman culture and the Latin language. How could it be "natural" and be so restricted? Or, from the other perspective, how could "common" law be based on arcane knowledge? Finally, from where did natural law come? It was not sufficient to say that it was created by God, for human reason was too. Rather, that argument created the problem of how such a created law could manifest itself in seemingly random historical circumstances that generated common law. One of the great appeals of Cartesianism was that it liberated the idea of reason from historical contingency and located it in the realm of the pure abstracting powers of the human mind. Thus the problem of fusing common law with natural law involved both epistemological and theological problems.

Vico's immediate attention was turned to defending both the tradition of humanist rhetoric and the tradition of common law. Shaftesbury's essay on *sensus communis* did not provide any direct information for such a defense, but it may have presented Vico with an agenda.

For Vico needed to show how *sensus communis* was developed by rhetorical education. In other words, he had to show how gentlemen of fashion could be fashioned, and why they should. And he had to do so with an eye on the defense of the common-law tradition. Shaftesbury's idea of *sensus communis* may have shown Vico what he had to explain and defend.

The sort of defense needed was a defense in the form of a synthesis: a theory that would unite common law and natural law in a way that would both guarantee access to them and locate their origin within history. Vico dedicated himself to finding this synthesis, and he created it out of the rhetoric he taught at the university, not rhetoric as a textually controlled discipline, but rhetoric as it was practiced in the Neapolitan courts and, indeed, in the courts of ancient Rome: primary rhetoric, used for extemporaneous oral performance. Vico addressed himself to finding the common ground of natural law and common law by exfoliating the epistemology implicit in oral rhetoric of Rome, Renaissance Italy, and his own Naples because it was that sort of rhetoric that made the law "practical" in the first place. Thus, he not only sought to unite common and natural law, but he also attempted to secure the relevance of the sort of university training he imparted to his students.

Vico's thought looks back to the traditions of fourteenth-century Italian humanism and its roots in Roman rhetoric to find a way to ground the *consensus* and defend natural and common law against their Cartesian opponents. *Sensus communis* became the conceptual ground on which Vico wished to build a synthetic view of law, but his idea of it begins with rhetorical practice, and he first began to develop that idea in his rhetorical, not his legal, writing.

3 Orality and Sensus Communis in Vico's Early Writings on Rhetoric

We have seen that Vico's Naples was intensely oral and adversative, divided into a multitude of classes and groups that competed for power by means of personal interaction and oral performance. We have also seen that the university accepted such a situation as normative and prepared its students to participate in it. Finally, we saw how the royal administration attempted to use Enlightenment philosophy as a rationale for reforming the university and the judicial system and thus consolidating its power on absolutist lines. Vico ultimately rejected Enlightenment philosophy and instead developed a theory of rhetoric as a response to its challenge.

In developing a theory of rhetoric that could stand up to the challenge of Cartesianism, Vico reached back to the classical and Renaissance roots of humanist rhetoric. When Vico went back to the classical and humanist rhetoricians, he read them with the model of oral performance in mind, the model with which he was best acquainted because it still obtained in Naples. He tried to give an account of how public speaking actually worked, how the orator actually composed an address. In those works he recovered a good deal of the latent orality that more print-oriented humanists had suppressed, and he used it to construct a performative theory of rhetoric that accounted for the way rhetoric and eloquence operated in his own milieu. In articulating this rhetorical theory Vico developed *sensus communis* as the rhetorical counterpart to Descartes' *bon sens,* and he developed it, as we shall see, as an essentially oral concept.

It is useful to distinguish what Vico meant by eloquence from what humanists such as Castiglione meant by it. *Sprezzatura,* a kind of

effortless effort or careless elegance, characterizes Castiglione's ideal
courtier, and rhetorical training aims to inculcate the linguistic equivalent, an ability to flatter, to charm, to speak wittily and gracefully
with just enough learning to impress one's hearers without intimidat-
ing them. Vico's idea of eloquence, however, is not characterized by
effortless effort, but by superhuman effort. In an address, *De mente
eroica,* delivered at the convocation beginning the academic year in
1732, he describes humanistic education as the acquisition and synthesis of all knowledge, a feat he compares to the great achievements
of the mythical heroes such as Hercules.[1] It is not *sprezzatura* that
characterizes Vichian eloquence but perspicacity, and rhetoric develops perspicacity, first, by teaching one how to select from memory
all the learning relevant to a particular situation, and second, how to
focus such learning on a particular case in an imaginative and effective
speech.

Vico began developing this rhetorical theory in his *Institutiones
oratoriae,* first published in 1711 and then revised and republished in
1738. The *Institutiones* was a textbook that Vico probably devised for
the rhetoric courses he taught at the university. It provides invaluable
information about how Vico taught rhetoric, as well as what he
thought about it. Two years before the *Institutiones* were published,
Vico published his *De nostri temporis studiorum ratione,* the inaugural
address that opened the university's academic year in 1708. In that
address he defended humanistic education and asserted its superiority
to the rationalistic studies and pedagogy being imported from France.
In the oration he first develops a notion of *sensus communis,* but it is
better understood in the context of Vico's own rhetorical theory and
practice, a context supplied by his *Institutiones.*

The *Institutiones* reveal the extent to which Vico recovered the
original, oral matrix of rhetoric. That oral matrix becomes apparent
as we examine Vico's treatment of invention, disposition, and style,
especially the use of figures of speech.

Vico's treatment of invention in the *Institutiones* is noteworthy for
its length and organization. He gives pride of place to forensic, or
legal, oratory, which was, after all, his special interest, and which
played a major role in the conduct of eighteenth-century Neapolitan
society. Vico is primarily concerned with inventing arguments in legal

cases, and he spends most of the section on invention in a discussion of how the *topoi* help to do this.

The *topoi* are in fact a systematic way of discovering arguments about a case or subject. There are "special" *topoi* suited only to certain kinds of cases, and there are the "general" *topoi,* which may be applied to any subject whatever. Vico's list of the general *topoi* differs very little from that given by Cicero in his *Topica:* definition, genus/species, difference, corollaries, adjuncts, antecedents and consequents, contradictions, cause and effect and, finally, comparison *(Institutiones* 390–97). Both Vico and Cicero's lists, however, differ somewhat from Aristotle's in the *Rhetoric,* which includes such things as "word play" and "inward thoughts and outward show" as possible sources of arguments along with the more usual topics (1397a–1402b).

What is more important than the lists of *topoi* is the way Vico conceives their use. Ramist dialectic had prescribed using the *topoi* to "think up" arguments and then prescribed "method" (a binomial logic) to sort them out and arrange them. Vico perceived that Aristotle's and Cicero's approach to the *topoi* was a good deal more sophisticated than that. Vico maintained Aristotle's original distinction between probability and certitude. Ramist dialectic had denied this distinction and asserted that the *topoi* could yield demonstrative proof. Vico held with Aristotle's distinction and thus developed his treatment of the *topoi* as sources of probability.

The basis of probable argument, for Aristotle, is common knowledge and accepted opinions *(Rhetoric* 1235a). Arguments from probability ultimately rest on "reputable opinion," what is "accepted by everyone or by the majority or by the wise—that is, by all, or by the majority, or by the most notable and reputable among them" *(Topica* 100b, 20–23). This is the ultimate foundation of an enthymeme, and the *topoi* are ways of appealing to it. Aristotle also gives some advice on how to appeal to it. One should not, he says, state every step in an argument *(Rhetoric* 1395b, 20–31), and he advises the orator to condense the enthymeme so that the audience will be compelled to supply some parts of the argument (1356a36–6b18, 1357a8–18).

While Vico held with Aristotle's notion of probable argument, his treatment of the *topoi* is also influenced by Cicero. Vico gives extensive treatment to the "special" topics, especially those dealing with forensic oratory, just as Cicero did in his *De inventione,* and later in the *Institutiones* Vico refers to the list of *topoi* in the *De oratore.* In his own list of the *topoi* Vico borrows his examples from Cicero, but he reshapes them significantly.

In the *De oratore* Cicero provided a list of topics, but each is specified by its relation to a case and then followed by an example. In other words, Cicero is careful to provide a context for each example: "If the argument turns on a word, remember Carbo's 'If a consul's duty is to consult the interests of his native land, what else has Opimius done?' " (II.xxxix, 165). Vico adopts Cicero's example, and his handling of it shows how he construes the relation of topic to argument. Carbo's statement in Latin is: "Si consul est, qui consulit patriae, quid aliud fecit Opimius?" Vico's Latin version is: "Consul fecit, non suo facto, consuluit Reipublicae" (The consul did it; he did not consult the republic in doing it). Vico has reversed the meaning of the enthymeme, heightening the word play on *Consul* and *consuluit,* and he has left the implied contradiction between being a consul and yet not consulting to be figured out by the audience. To this extent Vico has followed Aristotle's advice and left something to the audience, but in doing so he has constructed a peculiarly Roman sentence, a *sententia.* This connection between the *topoi* and the Roman tradition of the *sententia* is Vico's contribution to a theory of the topics.

Just how closely Vico saw this connection is illustrated by his continuing his treatment of the *topoi* and enthymemes in the *Institutiones'* section on metaphor. But before turning to that section let us look at how Vico handles disposition.

Both Ramism and Cartesianism taught that organization flowed out of the nature of the case according to a natural logic available to all who had good sense *(bon sens).* But Vico held to the old performance-dominated model of *dispositio* inherited from classical and early Renaissance rhetoric. Vico held that prudence actually determined a speech's organization, that is, the organization could depend upon external factors like audience and circumstance. We have seen how Aristotle wavered on this point, first asserting that a speech should have only two parts: stating the argument and proving it, and then proceeding to describe the four parts of an oration—proem, narration, proof, and peroration.

For Aristotle, *dispositio* is really a process of selection rather than of arrangement. The speech's structure provides a formal skeleton that specifies the sort of arguments that belong in each place. There is no discussion of arranging matter that has been discovered according to some sort of logic, except when dealing with propositional arguments themselves. Only these are governed by an internal logic; other arguments are suitable to other parts for external reasons, usually because of an effect upon an audience.

Aristotle's struggle to articulate a formal structure for *dispositio* independent of *inventio* does not inspire Cicero. In the *De partitione oratoria* (long attributed to Cicero), the author says bluntly that although arranging arguments belongs to both *inventio* and *elocutio,* it is really a part of *inventio* (313). Cicero then follows Aristotle's example in dividing the speech into four parts, but his analysis is free from the pressure to find a rigorous, formal derivation of these parts. Instead, Cicero maintains that they are invented along with the arguments themselves, or rather, *inventio* proceeds according to the demands of *dispositio:* "I adopt the whole method of arrangement to the purpose of the inquiry; for the purpose of the statement is to convince, and that of the case is both to convince and to excite emotion. Consequently when I have dealt with the case, which contains the statement, I shall have spoken of them both" *(De partitione* 319). Here the arrangement is adapted "to the purpose of the inquiry," which is to say, convincing. It is not derived from the *res.* A little later Cicero advises that "the prudent and cautious speaker is controlled by the reception given by his audience—what it rejects has to be modified" (323). *Dispositio* is controlled by performance.

When treating the various parts of the oration, Cicero gives the topics from which the most useful arguments for each section may be drawn. For example, in the argument and refutation (which like Aristotle he treats as one unit) he shows how inferences may be drawn from topics dealing with persons, for example, strength, beauty, age, circumstances of birth, offices, riches, friends—or the opposite of these *(De partitione* 339). In other words, the common topics of circumstances and relations are useful in drawing inferences about persons in the argumentative section of the oration. *Dispositio* is treated as a formal taxonomy of topics, the tendency Aristotle resisted in vain.

Cicero does present a formal analysis of the kind of questions an orator can address, for example, general or limited, and he does pay some attention to formal argumentation with an eye on the audience because the final test of an effective argument is its effect upon the audience. The same concern for effectiveness can be found in the section on arrangement in the *De oratore* (II:lxxvi–lxxxiii). Although he says at the outset that "there are two rules of procedure, one arising from the nature of the cases and the other contributed by the discretion and wisdom of the speakers," Cicero spends nearly all of the section on the latter—what the discreet and wise speaker should do in certain situations (II:lxxvi). Even when dealing with formal argument, judge or opposing speaker may make it prudent to deviate from a normal procedure.

Vico's approach to *dispositio* is far closer to Cicero in this regard than it is to Aristotle or Vico's late humanist predecessors. In the *Institutiones* Vico states that prudence should control the arrangement of a speech: "Disposition is two-sided: one is art, the other is prudence. . . . Prudence, which often deserts the precepts of art for the good of the case, transposes the parts of an oration, as when the arguments of the adversary have made an impression on the judge, we should begin with our confutation . . ." (42).[2]

He then proceeds to treat the traditional parts of an oration in turn, but always with an eye on the audience. This is not to say that Vico's treatment of *dispositio* is merely a study in flattery. Far from it. His treatment of confirmation is a thorough explication of how syllogisms and enthymemes can be drawn from the central proposition of the speech *(Institutiones* 56–66). The "logical" parts of the oration, the confirmation and confutation, he deals with in a logical manner, giving examples of formal argument from Cicero. But the other parts, including amplification, he treats as aimed at an audience, that is, their purpose is to move the emotions, to sway a verdict.

Vico's treatment of *dispositio,* like his treatment of *inventio,* focuses on forensic rhetoric. The arrangement of argument is controlled by prudence, although, obviously, a formally logical presentation has great potential for victory. Nonetheless, such argument is, in Vico's model, controlled by public oral performance in an adversarial situation. There is no question in Vico's rhetoric of argument being "disposed" according to formal principles, and certainly no question of its being arranged subsequent to some sort of random discovery.

Rather, even logical argument must be directed toward an audience, situation or opposition. Furthermore, as we have seen, this performance was, in Vico's own milieu, an extemporaneous one, or nearly so. How could the orator be logical and affective (and therefore effective) in such a situation? How could he discover and arrange material to achieve his purposes in such a public, oral, adversative, and *ex tempore* situation? Vico's response to this problem falls, amazingly enough, under his treatment of *elocutio,* style. In the heat of a public performance the pedagogical divisions of rhetoric cannot serve as sequential mental processes as Ramus and other later humanists conceived them. Rather, even *elocutio* (along with *inventio* and *dispositio*) must occur nearly simultaneously. Vico, in a flash of insight, solved the problem of describing how such argumentation can occur by synthesizing the classical notion of the *topoi* with the Latin *sententia* and the Baroque conceit. It was Vico's brilliant discovery that the finding of arguments, the focusing of them on the case and their stylistic expression, could be accounted for in one mental act, and it is in this synthesis that we find what Vico came to understand by *sensus.*

Vico discusses style in the last part of the *Institutiones* (90–130), but the treatment begins in a section entitled *De sententiis, vulgo del ben parlare in concetti* (Concerning sententiae, or in the vernacular, speaking in conceits) (90–101). Note that Vico is concerned with *speaking* in conceits, and that he equates the conceit with the *sententia.* Before proceeding it is important to understand each of these terms, *sententia* and *conceit,* which Vico is uniting.

We have already met *sententia* in our discussion of orality in classical rhetoric. The *sententiae* were part of the early training in grammar. They were short, pithy sentences, usually with a moral, which young boys memorized as part of their mastery of vocabulary and syntax. But Vico approached them from his background in jurisprudence as well as from his rhetorical background. For that reason they deserve some deeper study.[3]

Aristotle discussed a kind of *sententiae,* which he called *gnomai,* or maxims *(Rhetoric* 1394a19–1459a7). By these he meant general truths or "popular wisdom" used, usually, to clinch an argument. Their advantage, as Aristotle says, is that they put the argument in terms with which the audience already agrees, and which the audience will be happy to see used because it confirms their own sense of rightness when they see their own opinions invoked as general premises (1394a–95b). A secondary meaning for *gnomai* is "witty sayings" (in Greek, *ta asteia)*, an acute saying that instructs the audience and makes something easy to understand. From such quick learning the audience derives pleasure. The most accomplished kind of witty saying is the conceit Aristotle discussed as a form of metaphor, the "proportional" comparison: *A* is to *B* as *C* is to *D*. Aristotle's example, which Vico develops in the *Institutiones*, is "The shield of Bacchus" as a metaphor for a wine cup or the "bowl of Ares" for a shield *(Rhetoric* 1407a), that is, the wine cup is to Bacchus as the shield is to Ares. Thus for Aristotle the *gnomai* could be either proverbs or witty sayings, one type of which was the conceit, or proportional metaphor.

In Roman rhetoric the *sententia* became the clinching of an argument via a memorable or witty saying, usually a highly condensed philosophic statement. The most comprehensive treatment of *sententiae* in Roman rhetoric is Quintillian's:

> When the ancients used the word *sententia,* they meant a feeling or opinion. The word is frequently used in this sense by orators, and traces of this meaning are still found in the speech of every day. For when we are going to take an oath we use the phrase *ex animi nostra sententia* . . . and when we offer congratulations, we say that we do so *ex sententia.* . . . The ancients indeed, often expressed the same meaning by saying that they uttered their *sensa:* for they regarded *sensus* as referring merely to the sense of the body. But modern usage applies *sensus* to concepts of the mind, while *sententia* is applied to striking reflexions *[lumina]* such as are more especially introduced at the close of our periods. . . . (II:viii, v)

Later Quintillian says that the term *sententia,* in its oldest and most correct usage, refers to an aphorism, or in Greek, a *gnome,* and he adds that "Both the Greek and the Latin names are derived from the fact that such utterances resemble the decrees or resolutions of public bodies" (II:viii, v).

The most important points about Quintillian's treatment of *sententiae* are their relation to sensation *(sensus)* as well as to intellection, and their roots in public pronouncements (sentences). The first characteristic suggests a relation between concept and image, whereas the second suggests the public, commonly accepted opinion that Aristotle called "common sense" but Quintillian traces to some authoritative pronouncement. Vico explicates the relation of these two meanings, and he does so by placing the *sententiae* in the context of the Baroque conceit. While Aristotelian and Roman rhetoric treated the *sententiae* (or *gnomai*) as ornaments or arguments, an entirely different tradition, springing from Aristotle's *Poetics,* had developed about the aesthetic status of metaphor. That tradition flowed into the whole aesthetic and literary phenomenon called the Baroque.[4]

The Baroque tradition, within which Vico situated the classical rhetorical treatment of metaphor, was the tradition of *acutezze,* or wit. To Baroque poets like Marino, Donne, and Herbert, and to Baroque theorists like Gracian, Tesauro, Sforza-Pallavicino, and Peregrino, wit meant combining two apparently dissimilar things into a metaphor that highlighted a heretofore unnoticed similarity.[5] Aristotle's "proportional metaphor" became more highly prized as the terms of the proportion were more seemingly discordant. A Baroque conceit should strike its reader with both its novelty and its aptness; in short, the beholder or reader considered first how anyone could have thought of such a comparison, and then (if it were a successful conceit) how he could have missed it. This experience, said the poets and the critics, constituted aesthetic truth.

Baroque *acutezze* was subjected to a rigorous critique by French critics like Dominique Bouhours, who operated on Cartesian principles of methodic doubt and critical analysis. By their lights, wit's claim to yield truth was spurious. This dispute over Baroque poetics forms the immediate background of Vico's treatment of metaphor in the *Institutiones,* and the Baroque notion of wit becomes, in Vico's hands, the mode of uniting metaphor with the *sententiae* and the *topoi.*

To see what Vico and Baroque theoreticians were defending, and what French critics were attacking, consider a typical Baroque conceit: John Donne's well-known compass conceit from his "Valediction: Forbidding Mourning." He compares his and his lover's souls to a compass:

If they be two, they are two so
As stiff twin compasses are two;
Thy soul, the fixed foot, makes no show
To move, but doth, if the other do.

And though it in the center sit,
Yet when the other far doth roam,
It leans and hearkens after it,
And grows erect, as that comes home.

Such wilt thou be to me, who must,
Like the other foot, obliquely run;
Thy firmness makes my circle just,
And makes me end where I begun.

While one does not immediately perceive any basis for the equation—
lovers' souls equals geometer's compass—in Donne's hands it becomes a delicate and moving image. The image makes sense in spite
of appearing to be nonsense.

Italian and French critics were divided on whether such "making
sense" constituted truth. The Italians asserted the affirmative. They
claimed that in finding such an image the ingenuity (wit conceived as
a faculty) by-passed usual ratiocinative processes and seized upon a
truth in a way that fused logical certitude with aesthetic beauty. The
French responded that such truth was more easily ascertained by
logical processes, and that these processes themselves, when ade-
quately reflected in writing, constituted an aesthetic charm superior
to such metaphor. If metaphor was employed it must be employed
transparently so that the logical force of the assertion would be visible
through the aesthetic form. Bouhours, in his *La Manière de bien penser
dans les ouvrages d'esprit* (1771) expressed the French position: "thoughts
are more or less true to the extent that they more or less conform to
their object. The entire conformity constructs what we will call the
precision of thought, that is to say, just as clothes are well fitted
when they are perfectly proportioned to the person who wears them;
thoughts are precise *[justes]* also when they accord perfectly to the
things they represent" (42).[6]

Earlier in the same work Bouhours had said "Metaphors are like
transparent veils which allow us to see what they cover; or like carnival
masks under which one recognizes the person disguised" *(La Manière*
17).[7] This is the typical Enlightenment position that metaphor is a
figural use of a proper meaning, the proper meaning being the one
that accords precisely to thought and is perceptible under the "veil"
of metaphor.

Beneath this aesthetic concern was a deeper philosophical problem: the issue of whether ingenuity worked independently of cognitive processes, or whether it was simply another name for apprehension. If the latter, then one could hardly avoid admitting that the truth claims a conceit could make might as well be made by deductive logic. The aesthetic quality of the conceit remained separate from its truth claim, mere icing on the intellectual cake. The Italian Baroque theorists failed to establish ingenuity as a mental *faculty* and hence failed to establish its status as a truth-finding *activity*. As Joseph Mazzeo has summarized their predicament:

> Although the theorists tried to distinguish *ingegno* [ingenuity] from intellect, they always finished up by finding a kind of intellectual truth in conceit. This was a logical conclusion drawn from their purely intellectualistic definition of the conceit itself. As long as the product of the *ingegno* was defined in exclusively intellectualistic terms, there was scant hope of considering this *ingegno* a faculty divorced from the intellect and its operations. The inability to distinguish between the function of metaphor in poetry and the function of metaphor in philosophy and science is at the root of this dilemma. The attempted solution of this problem introduced a modified notion of the *ingegno* as a kind of creative or super intellect distinct from ratiocinative intellect. (1964, 49–50)

The Baroque conceit was a product of *letteraturizzazione*. Aristotle's description of the proportional metaphor in the *Rhetoric* and the *Poetics* became consciously adapted to the writing of poetry, poetry that strove after the effects Aristotle described. But Vico, as the product of his oral milieu, saw the conceit as performance controlled and emerging directly from the performer's grasp of certain similarities within the case. In short, Vico transferred the Baroque conceit from secondary rhetoric back to primary rhetoric.

In the *Institutiones* Vico describes conceits as consisting of three facets: words, things, and the ligamen, or connection, between them. The ligamen may be sensible or intelligible, and the intelligible ligamen may be either simple or complex. Vico describes how a conceit works and explicitly connects it to the enthymeme: "In a conceit with a complex intelligible ligamen, two ideas are yoked by means of a third which is either expressed or silent; this 'third thing' is the work of our mind and is called a syllogism by dialecticians but by rhetoricians an enthymeme" *(Institutiones* 91–92).[8] This definition is drawn from Book II of Aristotle's *Rhetoric* (1410b); Vico, however, adapts this notion of conceit-as-enthymeme to his own practice of *speaking in conceits,* and, in the process, he collapses the distinction between poetic and rhetorical uses of metaphor. First he describes conceits in Aristotelian terms drawn from both the *Rhetoric* and the *Poetics:* "acuity consists of a rare and novel aptness of two extremes happily juxtaposed in one statement. Such a discovery is extremely difficult, as Aristotle judged in *Poetics* where, in the argument about metaphor, he says it is only with the greatest difficulty that suitable metaphors (translations) are made and only with great flexibility of wit, and as he says in the *Rhetoric,* only the wisest and most acute philosophers are able to distinguish what similarity can be perceived in diverse things" *(Institutiones* 93).[9]

Vico also collapsed the distinction between rhetorical metaphor and poetic metaphor by invoking the Renaissance notion of "teaching and delighting." Vico says that the conceit combines truth and beauty, that it teaches and delights simultaneously. He also says that the conceit is created by the orator, not the poet: "The orator, in presenting an acute saying, makes beauty which is left to the hearer to discover; for it is present by virtue of the rational connection (ligamen) which, when the hearer discovers it, unites the extremes to allow for the contemplation of the similarity and thus reveals the beauty which the orator brought to pass. Thus the hearer seems ingenious to himself and the acute saying is delightful because it is more known by the hearer than presented by the speaker" *(Institutiones* 95).[10]

Vico's description of the conceit is controlled by his model of oral performance. The *hearer* participates in the metaphor when he seizes upon the ligamen, and thus unites what is learned with how it is learned. The discovery of the connection is both the source of beauty and truth. This act is, for Vico, aural.

The unification of teaching and delighting in oral performance moves Vico out of the problematics of Baroque aesthetic theory, but his next assertion in the *Institutiones* shows how rhetorical, and how oral, his conception of metaphor is. Vico addresses the author (then unknown to him) of *L'arte di ben pensare [sic]* and asserts that acute sayings or conceits find their source in the topics enumerated by Cicero in his *De inventione (Institutiones* 96). Here Vico claims that metaphor is the fruit of rhetorical invention, and, as every student knew, invention meant inventing arguments. In short, Vico claims that metaphor has the same source as argument. "Earlier, when discussing invention, Vico had said: "The argument then is a reason taken from some place, which is then applied to the thing under discussion in order to explicate it. The place is thus that from which one takes an argument. Thus the place is the house of argument, and its seat" *(Institutiones* 9).[11]

Attacking Bouhours frontally, Vico shows how paradox and symbol reveal truth. The audience discovers the truth when it perceives the ligamen connecting the terms of the metaphor. For example, Vico says, when Cicero called Rome "the fortress of the world," he united both the notion that Rome was a stronghold against the world and a stronghold for the world, that is, a refuge. Hence, the audience is persuaded of a truth about Rome's stature because they have discovered a connection between Rome's strength and its benevolence. This is the connection which, Vico says, makes the figure beautiful and true *(Institutiones* 96–97).

Thus, Vico claims that conceits are arguments, that they teach by uniting beauty and truth in an oral performance. The orator creates the conceit by the force of his ingenuity working on the case at hand. The audience seizes it as simultaneously true and beautiful. The truth is a rhetorical truth, addressed to the case, the audience and the situation at hand. There is no question of a "clear" argument with the mere addition of a decorative figure. The metaphor is the argument. Hence, Vico could say that metaphors could be drawn from Cicero's topics.

Vico unites the topics, *sententiae,* and the conceit into a single performative act. The orator creates an argumentative metaphor by constructing a proportional metaphor whose ligamen is one that the hearer discovers and recognizes as a truth he already believes. The orator must use the common sense of the audience as that which connects his metaphor to the case. The ligamen of the metaphor becomes the premise of the enthymeme. Hence "what is believed by all or most" is recovered by the audience in a new way, one that flatters their opinion (because it is their opinion that is discovered) and their opinion of themselves (it is they who discover it). They have found the sense the orator made, and discovered that it was their own. The metaphor is thus an argument because it makes a predication based on probability, a *sententia* because it clinches the case authoritatively, and a conceit because it delights its hearers. Thus the probable becomes convincing; the argument moves.

Classical rhetorical theory revealed that there were at least two possible roots for *sensus communis:* Aristotle's—what is held to be true by all, by most, or by the wisest—and Quintillian's—a public utterance or "sentence" traced to *sensus*, feeling, or opinion. Thus *sensus* for Vico had the dual meaning that sense still retains in English, a feeling or sensation, and an intellectual grasp on an idea, that is, "making sense." In his treatment of the conceit Vico intertwines these two linguistic roots into a concept of metaphor as argument. In the *De nostri temporis studiorum ratione,* he cultivates those roots to produce a theory of *sensus communis,* and, along the way, gives a phenomeno-logical account of how the mind's faculties operate to produce a convincing oral performance. Vico addresses the role of rhetoric (and perforce *sensus communis)* in the life of society. The *communis* as well as the *sensus* must be explained and defended.

ORALITY AND *SENSUS COMMUNIS* IN THE *DE NOSTRI TEMPORIS STUDIORUM RATIONE*

In the *De nostri,* Vico defends the humanist ideal of eloquence as an educational objective superior to the critical intellect that the Cartesian method aimed to produce. To mount this defense Vico had to do something that no other humanist had to do: explain how rhetorical training affected the mind, how it equipped the orator to find and articulate truth in the public sphere. An account of how the rhetorically trained mind worked had never been attempted because, before Des-cartes, no other competing philosophy had ever given a rival account that gained any influence in education. Vico's model for the interaction of ingenuity, fantasy, and *sensus communis* emerges from his contro-versy with Descartes.

Vico defends the necessity of eloquence, and therefore of an ability to reason from probability, for human life by introducing *sensus com-munis,* ingenuity, and fantasy into his general defense of eloquence. He then proceeds to defend rhetoric as the proper training for acquiring the skills in probability necessary for eloquence. Vico immediately

locates the crucial difference between humanistic education and Cartesian method: the former is based on the ability to reason to probable
truths; the latter employs systematic doubt: "Philosophical criticism
is the subject which we compel our youths to take up first. Now, such
speculative criticism, the main purpose of which is to cleanse its
fundamental truths not only of all falsity, but also of the mere suspicion
of error, places upon the same plane of falsity not only false thinking,
but also those secondary verities and ideas which are based on probability alone, and commands us to cleanse our minds of them" *(De
nostri* 13).

Vico then introduces *sensus communis* as arising from perceptions.
"Such an approach [Cartesian] is distinctly harmful, since training in
common sense is essential to the education of adolescents, so that faculty
should be developed as early as possible; else they break into odd or
arrogant behavior when adulthood is reached. It is a positive fact that,
just as knowledge originates in truth and error in falsity, so common
sense arises from perceptions based on similitude. Probabilities stand,
so to speak, midway between truth and falsity. . . ." *(De nostri* 13).

Cartesian method and rhetoric differ radically in their attitudes
toward probability. Cartesian method disvalues probability and thus
stifles *sensus communis,* which itself arises from the perceptions of such
similitude. "Arises" here is *gignitur* from *gignere,* to beget, bear, or
produce, the root of *ingenium.* Vico sees this "arising" as an active
perception, an ingenious discovery. When this activity is stifled, "odd
or arrogant behavior" may result. Vico continues: "Consequently,
since young people are to be educated in common sense, we should
be careful to avoid that the growth of common sense be stifled in
them by a habit of advanced speculative criticism. I may add that
common sense, besides being the standard of practical judgment, is
also the guiding standard of eloquence" *(De nostri* 13).

Sensus communis is a standard both of practical judgment and of
eloquence. The question arises of how this standard is derived from
"perceptions based on similitudes." Vico's answer introduces another
key term: *phantasia,* or fantasy.

Our modern advocates of advanced criticism rank the unadulterated
essence of "pure," primary truth before, outside, above the gross
semblances of physical bodies *[corporum immagines]* [*sic*]. . . .

Just as old age is powerful in reason, so is adolescence in imagination *[phantasia]*. Since imagination has always been esteemed a most favorable omen of future development, it should in no way be dulled. Furthermore, the teacher should give the greatest care to the cultivation of the pupil's memory, which, though not exactly the same as imagination, is almost identical with it. . . . Youth's natural inclination to the arts in which imagination or memory (or a combination of both) is prevalent (such as painting, poetry, oratory, jurisprudence) should by no means be blunted. (*De nostri* 14)

Here Vico states that the "gross semblances of physical bodies" are the object of the fantasy which, he says, is "almost identical" with memory. The chain of Vico's reasoning leads from *sensus communis,* a standard both of eloquence and practical judgment, developed by perceptions based on similitude, to the ground of these perceptions in corporeal images that are the object of fantasy, a faculty almost identical with memory. In following these connections one must remember that Vico is arguing against Cartesian method. The "gross semblances of physical bodies" are opposed to the "unadulterated essence of 'pure' truth." Vico made the same contrast in the *Institutiones oratoriae,* when he says: "let him [the student] learn geometry through forms in order that in one act he might acquire the art of arranging and, with the help of the fantasy (as boys tend to do), he might become accustomed to determining truth" (7).[12] By geometry "through forms" Vico means Euclidean geometry, as opposed to Descartes' analytical geometry, which operates exclusively with equations independent of visual representation of figures.

Vico's *Institutiones* illuminates the passage in *De nostri temporis studiorum ratione.* Vico describes the proper training of the fantasy. Rather than " 'pure' primary truth" that eschews "gross semblances of physical bodies," Vico calls for a "sensual" training of the fantasy, one that immerses it in images and rhythms. As he says in the *Institutiones:* "And I wish that a boy be imbued with that music called 'practical' so he might develop an ear for harmony to judge meters whether poetical or oratorical . . ."(8).[13]

The line of Vico's thought thus extends from a common sense rooted in probability, to probabilities founded on the perception of similitudes, which perceptions "arise" from a fantasy trained to remember in terms of visual and auditory experiences. Just how all this works is Vico's model of the effects of rhetorical training.

Vico locates in rhetorical training the source of that harmony and proportion Shaftesbury had called the essence of taste and the moral sense. Shaftesbury had said that this taste or sense was the hallmark of the "man of fashion" and could be acquired by education or possessed through "natural genius." Vico tries to determine just what in rhetorical education produces that sense and what sort of genius, or ingenuity, it requires. Vico, I believe, is tracing the formation of the moral sense by means of the oral performance on which his model of rhetoric is based.

The model is fashioned on eloquence, but eloquence is thus ultimately related to the physical. Vico accuses Cartesian method of substituting a private, discarnate mathematical model of human reason for the corporeal model of humanism, that is, humanistic education aimed at an "embodied" wisdom. These two ideals become the poles of Vico's debate with Descartes.

Vico proceeds to defend the humanistic ideal of wisdom by contrasting two aspects of rhetoric, *inventio* and *elocutio,* with the two main characteristics of Cartesianism, critical method and geometric logic. In his defense of *inventio* Vico contrasts the *topoi* with critical method, and in defending *elocutio* he contrasts the figures of speech with geometric logic. In each part Vico shows how probability operates within the rhetorical "art."

Vico first turns his attention to the process of invention, and he contrasts the mental processes involved in using the *topoi* with those involved with critical doubt:

> In our days, we keep away from the art of inventing arguments, and think that this skill is of no use. We hear people affirming that, if individuals are critically endowed, it is sufficient to teach them a certain subject, and they will have the capacity to discover whether there is any truth in that subject. It is claimed that, without any previous training in the *ars topica,* any person will be able to discover the probabilities which surround any ordinary topic, and to evaluate them *by the same standard employed in the sifting of truth.* But who can be sure that he has taken into consideration every feature of the subject on hand? (*De nostri* 14–15)

The *topoi* insure comprehensive treatment of a subject. Vico says later in the *De nostri:* "Criticism is the art of speaking truly, topics of speaking copiously" (15).[14] Thus to be "topical" is to be "copious."

Vico had said earlier "common sense arises from perceptions based on similitude. Probabilities stand, so to speak, midway between truth and falsity." The "arising" was an ingenious process. If one assumes "probabilities" to mean probable arguments, then one can say that the *topoi* are a method by which ingenuity can exhaust the probable arguments on a subject, and *copia* is the store of words and experiences upon which ingenuity works. One can go further and say that *copia* enters the mind and is held there by the fantasy, which Vico said was almost the same as memory and was to be encouraged by poetry, painting, and oratory. The *topoi* constitute a method by which ingenuity operates upon experience as it has been "incorporated" by the fantasy and kept "to hand" as *copia* in order to formulate probable arguments. The perceptions of these probabilities then would "give rise" to *sensus communis*.

Thus the *topoi* serve Vico as a method of discovery, a method both "ingenious" and pre-logical, which assumes that the mind can formulate premises congruent to experience and thereby keep the deductive process related to the real world. That relation is not grounded logically, but rather grounds logic in experience, the experience of seeing innumerable similarities in things and events and basing probable judgments on these similarities. To formulate such probable judgments requires "common sense," quite another thing from Descartes' *bon sens,* which discriminates logical steps rather than sees similarities in experience. Yet there remains the problem of the relation of experience to its linguistic expression: how is the perception related to its linguistic expression, or to language itself?

Vico addresses the role of language in *sensus communis* in his treatment of *elocutio.* In this second part Vico argues for the superiority of the tropes, the figures of speech, over Descartes' analytic logic. Once again Vico sees the conflict as one between attitudes toward similitude: "Our [Cartesian] theory of physics (in the process of learning as well as when mastered) moves forward by a constant and gradual series of small steps. Consequently, it is apt to smother the student's specifically philosophic faculty, i.e., his capacity to perceive the analogies existing between matters lying far apart and, apparently, most dissimilar. It is

this capacity which constitutes the source and principle of all ingenious, acute, and brilliant forms of expression" (*De nostri* 24).

Just as criticism hindered the invention of probable arguments, so
too much emphasis on logical distinction hinders the perception of
analogies that lead to figures of speech. This perception of analogies
is what Vico calls the "student's specifically philosophic faculty,"
and Vico proceeds to relate it to metaphor: "That which is tenuous,
delicately refined, may be represented by a single line; 'acute' by
two. Metaphor, the greatest and brightest ornament of forceful and
distinguished speech, undoubtedly plays the first role in acute, figurative expression" (*De nostri* 24).

This description of metaphor is peculiarly dense. "Acuity" is being
contrasted with "tenuousness," a term that Vico, in a passage of
the *Institutiones,* associated with the "science of numbers," saying
"tenuous things are deadly to oratory."[15] Here "tenuous" seems to
refer to simple linear progression, whereas acuity refers to two lines
focused upon a point. Hence metaphor is the "perception based on
similitudes," only now considered as originating figures of speech
rather than arguments.

How do the three faculties of *sensus communis,* ingenuity, and fantasy
operate in the making of a metaphor? Once again the *Institutiones* give
valuable information: "Ingenuity is necessary for contriving an acute
saying which, as sharply as possible, goes to the heart of the matter
to which it pertains and includes everything which pertains to the
affair and unifies them felicitously. Ingenuity is also necessary for deft
explanations in which things are beheld in conceits (and the words in
the conceits) more transparently than if seen through glass . . ." (5).[16]
Ingenuity creates acuity by unifying disparate elements into conceits,
sententiae. But ingenuity also keeps the figure felicitously suited to the
case at hand.

Recall the passage in the *Institutiones* where Vico explains how
ingenuity works to create acute metaphors: "This power of ingenuity
. . . consists in the yoking of different things: for in an acute saying
three things are discovered: the thing, the words and the ligature"
(91).[17] It is the ligature, Vico continues, which is the source of argumentative power. In a passage of the *Institutiones* already cited he calls
these ligatures intellectual and says that they can unite two ideas and
are called syllogisms by dialecticians but enthymemes by rhetoricians.

Here Vico is developing a geometric metaphor for how a conceit can be an argument. He seeks to illustrate the mental processes that serve to create the kind of argumentative metaphor he described in the *Institutiones*.

The illustration takes the form of a pun on *acutezze,* the acute or witty conceit is formulated like an acute angle. The two terms of the metaphor are joined by a point, the ligamen, which in turn is focused on the case in an "acute" expression. Vico contrasts this form of expression with Cartesian reasoning. The latter, he says, proceeds in a "single line." Acuity proceeds "by two." The two lines are, obviously, the two dissimilar things a metaphor "twins," and they are brought to a single point by the ligamen connecting them.

Vico's acute angle is analogous both to Donne's compass conceit and to the use of the acute angle in Baroque painting. In Tintoretto's "Last Supper," for example, perspective is organized on an acute angle to focus attention upon a dramatic gesture, thus capturing a moment of time. The table at which Christ and the Apostles are sitting extends in an acute angle from the horizontal of the picture plane. The viewer of the painting is pulled into the scene along the line of the angle and thus becomes a participant; so, too, the hearer of an acute metaphor or conceit is involved in the argument by discovering the implied ligamen. Vico's image is one of penetration, an image in three dimensions in which metaphor creates an interior and penetrates it, taking the hearer along.

While Cartesian critics like Bouhours separated ratiocination from aesthetics, Vico's description of metaphor features the simultaneous creation and interpenetration of aesthetic and argument. The description relies on a model inherited from Baroque aesthetics, a model that features simultaneity, interiority, and insight. Vico not only denies that metaphor is a decorative figure on a logical presentation, but he also asserts that metaphor is superior to the unadorned logic of Cartesian method.

The simultaneity of argument and figural expression can be traced to the necessity for speaking *ex tempore* and the rhetorical training that fitted one for it. Vico says in the *De nostri:*

In pressing, urgent affairs, which do not admit of delay or postponement, as most frequently occurs in our law courts—especially when it is a question of criminal cases, which offer to the eloquent orator the greatest opportunity for the display of his powers—it is the orator's business to give immediate assistance to the accused, who is usually granted only a few hours in which to plead his defense. Our experts in philosophical criticism, instead, whenever they are confronted with some dubious point, are wont to say: "Give me some time to think it over." (15).

In an oral performance the process of argument and expression is compressed into a single act and is not divided into the stages of development through which a written composition usually proceeds. Vico's description of *sensus communis,* ingenuity, and fantasy proceeds according to his view of how the orator creates effective arguments in that concrete situation.

The orator's power of effective persuasion depends not only on the logical force of the argument, but also upon the nuances within the language that constitutes the figure in which the argument is couched. For example, by comparing the act of drinking to Bacchus' shield, the orator forces the interpenetration of the affective associations of the words "Bacchus' shield" and "drinking," associations he has interiorized in his training. This interpenetration generates the possibility of other similitudes. The similitude is perceived linguistically insofar as affective meanings cluster around words that carry an indeterminate set of resonances, some shared by the entire language community, some by a part of the community, and some peculiar to each individual and derived from personal experience. But the orator, ideally at least, has not only perceived the similitude, but he also understands the shared meanings; he perceives how the words in the figure will resonate together in the language. When an orator constructs a metaphor, he should use the pre-logical, affective power of language because he has consciously interiorized that power in his fantasy. These meanings are what fantasy "incorporated," the feel of the *imagines corporum,* the rhythm of the language, in short, the somatic nature of language. When those meanings, along with the comprehensive vocabulary they support, are available to the ingenuity, they constitute *copia.*

The persuasive power of any figure depends on the perception of the similarity between the terms, and a similarity between that similarity and the case at hand. Furthermore, it depends upon the fact that the orator has a sufficient grasp of the affective power of language. The ability to use this power presupposes that the orator has interiorized it, that he is aware of commonly shared, affective pre-logical meanings, images, and rhythms. The orator focuses these meanings on the case at hand in a way that fuses argumentative and aesthetic power.

To complete this account of *elocutio* and *inventio,* the "ground" of the shared meanings must be found. What is the ground of intelligibility shared by orator and audience, upon which their imaginations work to make persuasion happen? According to Vico, as we have seen, both *inventio* and *elocutio* are ingenious activities, both operate on the contents of the fantasy, and both depend upon the perception of similitudes. What is the basis of similitude that makes persuasion possible? How does the orator know which probability or figure will be most effective? The answer, I believe, is *sensus communis.* It is the sense made when an argumentative figure "makes sense" in a particular case. In other words, the argumentative figure invokes some shared meaning within the language and focuses it on some present situation so that the situation is understood by the audience; they understand it because the orator presents it "in terms of" a similitude they can recognize. That understanding is probable because the figure is, after all, a similitude, not an identity. The new situation is perceived as like something else, and thus action or decision is urged on the grounds of this probable familiarity.

To be effective, however, the audience must not only see the similarity, but they must also feel it in the emotional force of the figure. The orator, in short, invokes the pre-logical affective power that underwrites the ethical consensus of the community. But that sense has to be available to the orator, and he has access to it in the poetic nature of language, the "common sensuality" that the audience shares, and which embodies the *consensus.* It is at this level that the perceptions of similitude supply power to the argument. Learning to indwell this world and to incorporate it in his fantasy is the young orator's primary task. It is from this "unclear" and "indistinct" substratum that metaphor and the other tropes derive their force, and that force reinforces the civic community when it decides upon an action. *Sensus communis* is where the civic community embraces the language community.

The oral nature of *sensus communis* becomes clear when we remember, first, how orality dominated the rhetorical training in the classical and early Renaissance periods, and second, when we remember that extemporaneous oral performance was Vico's model of eloquence. In the first case, continuous oral performance and recitation furnished the young orator with *sensus communis* considered as the somatic aspect of language, its rhythm and feel. This aspect was interiorized simultaneously with the mores and values of the community that formed the content of fables, maxims, and *sententiae,* which the young orator memorized and imitated. This material was held in the fantasy as *copia,* but held as "oral memory" in a way analogous to the way in which the rhapsodes or the Sophists memorized formulas. When called upon to speak, the orator had to choose appropriate material from this fund and focus it upon the case at hand. Oral memory had to provide material for oral creation.

The second aspect, just how this ad hoc oral creativity functions during performance, displays the workings of *sensus communis.* For Vico, *sensus communis* means also the ability to perceive similarities between the contents of the fantasy and a new situation, hence the role of ingenuity in choosing and focusing the *copia* held in the fantasy. That ingenious activity forms probable arguments, arguing for a new state of affairs by noting its similarities to the old and invoking certain timeless values held by the community, "what is held by all or by most." Vico's notion of *sensus communis* differs from his predecessors in that he recognized that the orator interiorized that "common opinion" along with language training, and that the orator had to both argue from it and argue toward it. It was both the source of his eloquence and the goal of his eloquence, that which he hoped to foster in a new, practical case. As Vico said at the beginning of the *De nostri, sensus communis* is both the standard of practical judgment and the guiding standard of eloquence.

These two aspects of *sensus communis* are united when the orator composes a metaphor. Then the fantasy provides material from the *sensus communis*-as-*copia* that the ingenuity fuses with the new situation to represent the *sensus communis*-as-practical judgment. The first aspect is the *sensus* as both value and corporeal perception via language; the second is the *communis* as shared language and opinion. The metaphor twins these aspects and makes the ligamen between the terms of the metaphor a ligamen between the terms of an enthymeme. Hence Vico can refer to such metaphors as both conceits and *sententiae.* They are conceits because they are new visions of reality (or a vision of a new reality), and they are *sententiae* because their terms invoke accepted communal values imbedded in language. Thus the orator presents his case so that the audience perceives it to be grounded in the "sense of the community," a sense they discover when they discover the ligamen in the metaphor-enthymeme. He can lead the audience to make sense out of that particular case and persuade it to choose a particular course of action, which he presents as committing, or rather recommitting, it to certain values.

The way Vico's notion of *sensus communis* is grounded in the notion of community participation leads him to conclude his treatment of it with a ringing condemnation of Cartesianism: "Our young men, because of this training, which is focused on these studies [Cartesian science], are unable to engage in the life of the community, to conduct themselves with sufficient wisdom and prudence; nor can they infuse into their speech a familiarity with human psychology or permeate their utterances with passion" (*De nostri* 33–34)

Vico's distinction between rhetoric and Cartesian method is essentially a ethical one, based on a difference of value. Vico's view of human existence is one of "public life." By "life of the community," he means the participation in practical political affairs, the conflicts of interests and the lawsuits for which, in Vico's Naples, humanist rhetoric prepared its students.

Vico's model of the mind is a model that works in that milieu, a model of eloquence-as-performance. The mind deals with language in a public arena; it deals with a language the audience knows, with meanings they share, with the images and rhythms and emotions that support those meanings. The *sensus communis* keeps the individual rooted in the community and in the community's past as well. The individual acquires the *sensus communis* when fantasy embodies the aesthetic power imbedded in the language. Ingenuity brings the *sensus communis* to bear; it articulates that sense so that it includes the present in order to affect the future. The model is "holistic" in that the three faculties "circulate" language and reality through the mind and body and keep the individual rooted in past and in community.

In Vico's writings on rhetoric, *sensus communis* emerges as the epistemological basis for persuasion. It is what connects the trained orator's mind to the public sphere, and it is what he articulates and advances when he creates forceful, witty, and effective arguments. *Sensus communis* is interiorized orally and expressed orally. It is not just "what is held by all or by most." *Sensus communis* is more than a quality of argument. Rather, it is both a quality of language and a faculty that grounds and creates effective arguments. It is that quality that makes eloquence possible, and which rhetorical training seeks to imbue. In the *Institutiones oratoriae,* Vico revealed his commitment to an oral-performative idea of rhetoric, and he gave an account of how arguments and figures were created during extemporaneous performance different from the account derived from textually controlled post-Renaissance pedagogy. In the *De nostri,* Vico defended rhetoric and explored its epistemological basis. That basis he found to be *sensus communis,* a notion that fused the pre-logical, oral substrata of linguistic meaning with the way the individual imagination operates in extemporaneous performance. Together these two works give us Vico's view of how the human mind operates. In the *New Science,* he developed this model into an account of the origins and operations of human culture.

4 Sensus Communis *in the* New Science

Between the publication of the *De nostri* in 1709 and the publication of the first *New Science* in 1725, Vico published two major philosophical treatises, *De antiquissima italorum sapientia* (1710) and the *Il diritto universale*.[1] These two works reveal that Vico was moving toward finding a link between language and law, and they constitute the immediate background of the idea of *sensus communis* that he develops in the *New Science*.

The *De antiquissima italorum sapientia* is important, first, because in it Vico arrives at the *verum-factum* distinction, and, second, because in it he first perceives that language itself can reveal the network of meanings within which social institutions operate.

The *De antiquissima italorum sapientia* has been called the "strangest" of Vico's works (Mooney 1985, 191). It is a hodgepodge of metaphysics, etymology, and ethics. Vico wrote it to demonstrate that the etymology of Latin words revealed the Romans to have had philosophical subtlety equal to that of the Athenian philosophers. As a humanist response to the *Meditations,* it continues his polemic against Descartes, just as the *De nostri* was a response to the *Discourse on Method.* The major part of the work employs etymology to discover the philosophical underpinnings of Roman law and Roman society. Vico's etymological method was arcane, to be sure. The study of etymology was part of a humanist education, but for Vico, etymologies were, as Mooney suggests, "parts of a great puzzle, a means by which disparate items are bound together or things unknown produced from what is familiar or near at hand" (1985, 195). Such a concept, as Mooney notes, harkens back to the practice of the Roman jurisconsults, who sought for arguments rather than definitions in the origin of words (195). Vico speculates about how language operated to describe and circumscribe external reality, how it gives an account of how a language "made sense" out of sensations. The following passage from the *De antiquissima* exemplifies Vico's method: "The term *facultas* was pronounced *facultias* from which later arose *facilitas*, a kind of easy or ready skill, as it were, in doing things. Thus facility is that whereby a power is translated into an act. The soul is a power, vision an act, and the sense of vision a faculty. . . . On this matter the views of the ancient philosophers of Italy survive in the words *olere* [to smell of] and *olfacere* [to perceive by smelling], for *olere* is applied to things and *olfacere* to living beings, implying that living beings make smell by smelling" (67–68).

This sort of etymology leads Vico to one of his crucial insights: the *verum-factum* principle.

> Imagination is a true faculty, because in using it we create images of things. Internal sense is another such faculty, for in battle men feel pain [only] when, having withdrawn from it, they notice their wounds. Similarly, intellect is a true faculty since, when we understand something by the intellect, we make it true. Thus, arithmetic and geometry and their offspring, mechanics, lie within human faculties, since in them we demonstrate the true because we make it. Physics, on the other hand, lies within a faculty of Almighty God, in whom alone the faculty is true, because it is in the highest degree easy and ready, so that what is a faculty in man is purest act in God. (68)

Here Vico is asserting that the true *(verum)* can be known when the human mind makes it *(factum)*, the way the mind generates mathematical principles. But external reality, for example, physics, can only be known as true by God because He made it.

This distinction is directed at the Cartesians' attempt to use a mathematical model for reasoning about the external world. In the *Il diritto universale* Vico articulates another principle: the *verum-certum* principle. By the "certain," Vico means those particular decisions and judgments that a community makes, such as declaring war or honoring marriages. Such practical judgments are "made certain," that is, they are established and become *res gestae* (things accomplished), and as such they become true.

The *verum-certum* principle lies at the heart of Vico's *Il diritto universale*. This work is larger than the *New Science* and attempts to reconcile natural law with common, or historically produced, law. His argument runs counter to the theories of Grotius, Selden, and Pufendorf, who tried to ground natural law in a nonhistorical rationality.[2] The Romans distinguished between civil law *(lex)* and universal law *(jus gentium)*.[3] Civil law was the actual code of laws applied in any given society. Universal law was the common element in the laws of all civil societies. Vico accused Grotius, Selden, and Pufendorf of arguing that the universal law was the product of abstract thought, that is, that immutable law was conceived by human reason in a primitive society and then embodied in particular codes.[4] Vico criticized Grotius, Selden, and Pufendorf for "beginning in the middle," that is, they posited the rationality of law entering primitive society directly and without any preparation or cause. Donald P. Verene has summarized Vico's position as holding that the universal law is established by custom and is a reflection of the *sensus communis*. Universal law "emerges as the form of society itself and is the basis from which law is subsequently formed" (1981, 61). The universal law emerges from the conditions of primordial existence, which elicit similar responses from all societies rather than from a formulation of some rational ideal.

Guido Fasso (1976) argued that *Il diritto universale* started Vico on the road to a theory of human culture. He argues that Vico was concerned with synthesizing the relationship between natural law and historical, positive law. The *jus gentium,* or "natural law of the gentes," is true *(verum)* because it is universal. It is also *certum* because it is made, that is, it appears only in practice. Thus Vico is able to show how natural law can become common law through the *verum-certum* principle. Furthermore, the *Il diritto universale* points toward a reconciliation of the philosophical with the philological method.[5] In the *De antiquissima,* Vico had used etymology to reveal philosophical wisdom, so in the *Il diritto universale* he shows how philological investigations may reveal the network of judgments by which the *jus gentium* came to be embodied in a particular society. Guido Fasso has argued (1976) that it was not until the first version of the *New Science* that Vico saw the relation between the *verum-certum* principle articulated in *Il diritto universale* and the *verum-factum* principle articulated in the *De antiquissima* some twenty years earlier.

As Verene has noted, the *sensus communis* is what the community reflects upon in order to embody the *jus gentium* in practical codes (1981, 61). But what is the *sensus communis* before there is a *jus gentium?* Somehow Aristotle's definition, what is agreed upon by all or by most, is inadequate: How can it be what is agreed upon by all or most *before* there has been any agreement? The *New Science* answers this question by retracing the formation of universal law from practical judgment, and then reconstructing the linguistic and religious preconditions of such judgment.

SENSUS COMMUNIS AND JUDGMENT

The *New Science* bewilders those who read it for the first time, and by modern critical standards it is a hopelessly confused work, for Vico's style is as oral as his rhetorical theory. Despite the division of the text into five books plus a conclusion, Vico's method follows a kind of stream of consciousness controlled by verbal association rather than logical development. The *New Science* is a collection of paragraphs, each containing an insight or making a claim with aphoristic intensity. The text is frequently repetitious; some paragraphs reassert the same claim as paragraphs hundreds of pages earlier, but with different evidence or from another perspective. The arguments are frequently couched in conceits, the form of argument Vico valued most.

Vico first mentions *sensus communis* in the *New Science* as a ground of choice: "that which makes human choice certain with respect to needs and utilities" (141). It is the basis by which practical decisions are reached, and thus it makes choice certain, that is, *certum*. It provides the ground for value judgments about practical priorities and serves, as Verene points out, as the criterion that brings the *jus gentium* into play. Vico offers a definition of *sensus communis* in the next sentence: it is "judgment without reflection, shared by an entire class, an entire people, an entire nation, or the entire human race" (142). *Sensus communis* is quite pointedly not predicated of an individual, rather, it is judgment shared but unreflective. It is not self-conscious, nor is it, at this stage of the *New Science,* connected with language. It is simply a practical judgment concerning needs and utilities around which a community has formed a consensus.

In the next paragraph Vico asserts that *sensus communis* "along with the following definition will provide a new art of criticism for the founders of nations . . ." (143). He then states that "Uniform ideas originating among entire peoples, unknown to each other must have a common ground of truth" (144). Vico is here referring back to his work on universal law. The "uniform ideas" are the social values that ground each community and are found in every society, the *jus gentium,* or Vico's "natural law of the gentes." The idea of "common ground" extends both outward toward humanity and downward to "truth," the ground of commonly held values, and does not refer to the mere consensus of unreflective judgment but to the basis for the universality of that consensus. Once again, in contrast to Descartes, there is no mention of the individual; the uniform ideas are communal. The *sensus communis* is the "common ground of truth," and "truth" is the community's judgment about practical needs and choices, those things it "makes certain." *Sensus communis* is the criterion for social judgment: "This axiom is a great principle which establishes the common sense of the human race as the criterion taught to the nations by divine providence to define what is certain in the natural law of the gentes. And the nations reach this certainty by recognizing the underlying agreements which despite variations of detail obtain among them in respect of this law" (145).

Vico here summarizes the position he articulated in *Il diritto universale. Sensus communis* is a criterion taught to the nations by divine providence to enable them to "certify" those customs and laws found in every human community. They reach this certainty by recognizing the "underlying agreements" that must order social life if it is to be social at all.

Vico's statement raises the issue of just what these "underlying agreements" are and how they come into play. At one level they are the unreflective judgments. But Vico pursues the issue. He says that from these underlying agreements issue "the mental dictionary for assigning origins to all diverse articulated languages" (145). For the first time Vico introduces the notion of language in his treatment of *sensus communis* in the *New Science.*

SENSUS COMMUNIS, LANGUAGE, AND
THE IMAGINATIVE UNIVERSALS

In pursuing the linguistic aspects of *sensus communis,* Vico turns to the rhetorical meaning of the term as he had explored it earlier in his rhetorical writings. He refines the relation of language to community: "There must in the nature of human institutions be a mental language common to all nations, which uniformly grasps the substance of things feasible in human social life and expresses it with as many diverse modifications as these same things may have diverse aspects" *(New Science* 161).

If the natural law of the gentes is embodied in every human society, then there must be a common mental language, not a verbalized one necessarily, which grasps those needs and utilities and the ways to satisfy them. In other words, there must be some mode by which communities make their needs intelligible to themselves so that the community can make judgments about satisfying those needs and thus begin to give shape to the *jus gentium.*

Vico offers a proof of the existence of this "mental language": "proverbs or maxims of vulgar wisdom, in which substantially the same meanings find as many diverse expressions as there are nations ancient and modern" (161). This "vulgar wisdom" of proverb lore evidences that every language can equally yet uniquely express those judgments shared by the entire human race. For example, "Look before you leap" has its equivalent in other cultures, such as the Russian "Measure the cloth nine times before cutting it once." Proverbs illustrate how each community uses the *sensus communis* to arrive at particular and unique manifestations of the same natural law of the gentes. Nonetheless Vico has still not addressed the origin of the *sensus communis* except to say that it is taught to the nations by providence. He has not yet described how he thinks that occurs.

Vico begins the description with an account of the origins of poetry. Poetry, he says, begins with the first, crude men describing the exterior world in terms of their own body, as in the "brow of a hill" (236). Vico sees the progression of human language as follows: "fable, custom and its appropriateness; sentence; locution and its expressiveness; allegory; song; and finally verse" (235). Vico conceives what he calls "poetic theory" (235), or the progression of poetic development in human speech, as following the old and familiar stages of the progymnasmata. The sequence in which young boys learned poetry by heart is, Vico claims, the same sequence the human race follows when it proceeds from a state of feral nature to full speech. Because language begins with poetry, the poetry of metaphors drawn from the human body, Vico claims to have a "universal principle of etymology" that will reveal the sources of institutions and concepts to be in the properties of physical bodies. Vico concludes his "Statement of Principles" with the statement quoted above: for this inquiry, we must "reckon as if there were no books in the world" (330). Vico disavows what he calls the "conceit of the nations," each of which believes itself to be the first in the world, and the "conceit of scholars," who maintain that what they know must have been understood from the beginning (330).

Vico shares with Descartes an interest in creating a system that eschews Renaissance philosophy and goes back to origins. But although Descartes found his starting point in the meditative power of the individual mind, Vico finds his in the experience of primary, that is, oral, rhetoric. He rejects the work of his immediate predecessors because, not understanding what the primitive mind must have been like, they "read into" the past the qualities of reason derived from the interiorization of literacy. Instead of these "conceits," Vico plans to trace the origins of society out of the primary metaphors of language. What he is doing, in fact, is committing himself to reconstructing imaginatively the origins of primary, oral rhetoric and its relation to *sensus communis*, a task he undertakes in the next book, "The Poetic Wisdom."

LANGUAGE AND POETIC WISDOM

Vico begins his reconstruction of rhetoric's origins with metaphor because, as he says, that is where language began, and he describes language, religion, and human society originating in a vast metaphor, one drawn from the human body itself. This metaphor is, of course, his famous description of the giants becoming human by responding to thunder:

a few giants . . . were frightened and astonished by the great effect [lightning and thunder] whose cause they did not know, and raised their eyes and became aware of the sky . . . they pictured the sky to themselves as a great animated body, which in that aspect they called Jove, the first god of the so called greater gentes, who meant to tell them something by the hiss of his bolts and the clap of his thunder. And thus they began to exercise that natural curiosity which is the daughter of ignorance and the mother of knowledge, and which, opening the mind of man, gives birth to wonder. (*New Science* 377)

Vico's description of the *arche* of society/language/religion is itself a conceit. The giants note the similarity between their own shouts and roars and the sounds of the sky, and they attribute significance to the latter, that is, the sky is speaking to them. Jove is thus the ligamen connecting thunder and sky with body and voice. The perception of this similarity makes "thunder" a word and coincidentally creates a fable for its origin, Jove. The word and the fable coexist in the conceit and are born simultaneously with the perception of the ligamen, which constitutes the "truth" of this vast conceit. Vico continues:

The first men, who spoke by signs, naturally believed that lightning bolts and thunder claps were signs made to them by Jove; whence from *nuo,* to make a sign, came *numen,* the divine will, by an idea more than sublime and worthy to express the divine majesty. They believed that Jove commanded by signs, that such signs were real words, and that nature was the language of Jove. The science of this language the gentiles universally believed to be divination, which by the Greeks was called theology, meaning the science of the language of the gods. (379)

Vico's account of the giants not only claims to describe the *arche* of speech, but also of language. Once the giants perceive the metaphoric quality of thunder and posit its fabulous origin, they must interpret it. In Vico's account, language begins, not with men speaking, but with men listening. Their first linguistic act is not speech but hermeneutic, the interpretation of the thunder's meaning. They must "figure out" what Jove wants them to do. Vico then claims that the giants interpret the thunder as a warning against indiscriminate copulation. They flee into caves to escape Jove's wrath and thus form the first families. The metaphor gives birth not only to language, but also to judgment, the flight to the caves is the first *res gesta,* which certifies the truth of the divine message. Thus language, God, religion, and community are created simultaneously with the perception of this first metaphor.

Vico's term for this primal metaphor is *imaginative universal.* It is one of Vico's most significant concepts, one he says cost him the labor of nearly his whole life. "We find that the principles of these origins both of languages and of letters lies in the fact that the first gentile people, by a demonstrated necessity of nature, were poets who spoke in poetic characters. This discovery, which is the master key of this Science, has cost us the persistent research of almost all our literary life, because with our civilized nature we cannot at all imagine and can understand only by great toil the poetic nature of these first men" (34).

Vico defines the imaginative universals, of which Jove is the first example, as "poetic characters" or "imaginative genera." Within this concept lies the origin of the *sensus communis,* for it initiates those "underlying agreements" as well as the "mental dictionary."

In conceptualizing the "imaginative universal," Vico asks how mind has ideas of sense perception. The giants make noises, hear thunder, and experience emotions. But Jove is created when the giants transfer *(metaphrein)* those human qualities to the sky and see it as a vast body making angry noises. The giants attribute all human emotions to Jove; he becomes a metaphor that links human qualities with superhuman powers, human qualities that were not the object of self-consciousness until they became perceived outside the human and then reconnected to it metaphorically. In short, the human first became known as the divine, and as Vico points out, as something to be "divined," that is, as something to be interpreted. Perhaps the best way to understand the imaginative universals is to consider them as "imaginative class concepts" analogous to abstract class concepts or genera used in conventional definitions. Such "class concepts" are formed by the *phantasia,* that imaginative faculty that baroque aesthetics credited with the power of seeing similarities and combining images. Vico's point is that the original humans were incapable of conceptualizing intelligible genera. Rather, because their experience was emotional and their expressions poetic, that is, metaphorical, instead of creating logical genera, they created imaginative ones. All attributes of divinity were identified with Jove. Likewise, Achilles became the imaginative universal of bravery. Men who were brave were Achilles, not like Achilles, but actually him. Clever men were Odysseus (809). What we term bravery, courage, and honor were, to the ancient Greek, all subsumed under the imaginative class concept "Achilles." The character substituted for the qualities; those who had the qualities were perceived as "impersonating" the character.

Vico continues to state that the first men created many such imaginative class concepts, and that they served them as "imaginative topics. . . . The first founders of humanity applied themselves to a sensory topics, by which they brought together those properties or qualities or relations of individuals and species which were, so to speak, concrete, and from these created their poetic genera" (495).

Vico claims that the first man sought for sensory analogues between individual experiences or objects, for example, brow and hill, boiling and anger. From these identifications they created a set of imaginative genera according to which subsequent experiences could be identified: "And it [the human mind] first began to hew out topics, which is an art of regulating well the primary operation of our mind by noting the commonplaces that must all be run over in order to know all there is in a thing that one desires to know well, that is, completely" (496).

Primitive man used imaginative universals to interpret reality the way an orator would use the topics to investigate a case. The imaginative universals provided an "index" for classifying experience. Men could be perceived as "Achilles-like" or "Odysseus-like" before they were perceived as brave or clever. These concepts were more real than their particular manifestations. As Vico says, "The true warrior chief is that Godfrey whom Tasso imagined" (205). The poets create the real in which the particular participates and against which it is measured. Verene has summarized the difference between intelligible and imaginative universals:

The warrior does not conceive of his nature as apart from that of Godfrey, the true war chief. To the extent that he *is*, he and Godfrey have an identical reality. According to Vico's view, the distinctive characteristic of mythic or primordial thought is its power to assert *identities* not *similarities*. The intelligible universal came about through the development of the mind's ability to objectify experience through the discovery of similarities and differences in perceptual objects and the formulation of them in terms of common properties. The poetic mind structures experience through the formulation of immediate identities between elements. (1981, 75–76)

The imaginative universals provide a key with which to interpret physical reality, but their origin is also an interpretation, as Jove was an interpretation of thunder. The imaginative universals come into being because they are needed to deal with pressing emotions. They begin with thunder, trembling, and fear, or with triumph, violence, and death. The imaginative universal is thoroughly corporeal. It simply freezes sensation in a kind of stop-action and attributes it to someone or something else. The metaphorical translation thus effected allows men to make sense out of their sensations, to objectify them in ways that both constellate a meaningful interpretation of external reality and generate a level of self-consciousness of sensation itself.

The imaginative universal is an expanded version of the Baroque conceit, which Vico claimed in his *Institutiones oratoriae* could couch an argument. Jove is the ligamen of a metaphor that makes a case, which argues for certain behavior. The imaginative universal is also, as Vico says, a fable. Jove is "fabulous" in that he explains or fuses the phenomena of thunder and sky with the human body and its noises. For Vico, Jove is a "true" story in that his existence "makes true" the actions the giants undertake in response to his word. Vico traces the word *logos* to mean *fable,* which is equivalent to *myth* which, he says, means in Latin a *vera narratio,* a true story (401).

The imaginative universal fuses the origin of language, religion, and community in a metaphor that organizes and interprets sense data. As such, it constitutes the origin of the two aspects of *sensus communis:* "underlying agreements" (e.g., the decision to go to the caves) and the "mental dictionary" (e.g., the fable of Jove). The imaginative universal "makes certain" the decision and the fable because both occur simultaneously, each ratifying the other. This ratification occurs even before the appearance of spoken language and, in fact, makes that appearance possible. The imaginative universal creates human self-consciousness by suspending the flux of sensation, fixing sensation in time and projecting it onto external reality.

Finally, the imaginative universal finds its origin in the numinous. The thunder apprehended as of divine origin is the *mysterium tremendum et fascinans;* it provoked the fear that in turn stimulates the metaphoric leap and its subsequent community-forming interpretation. Vico attributes this religious event to Divine Providence. By imploding the *arche* of language, religion, and community into one imaginative act, Vico provides the *sensus communis* upon which *jus gentium* operates. This *sensus communis* is a "common sense" in a very literal and strict sense: the community learns to arrest its sensations, perceive them, and respond to them as a community. From this original imaginative universal, Jove, come others that advance the community's self-understanding and certify its social institutions by providing a "sensory topics" that organize and interpret other, more complex sense perceptions. These other universals likewise originate in a poetic act, one that establishes identities between exterior reality and the metaphor or mythos. Such images become, like Jove, true fables that fuse sensation, affection, and action to certify as true the reality they reflect and create. Reality becomes that with which the poetic image is identifiable, that which participates in it. The imaginative universal, then, provides the "given" out of which the first humans gave form to the *jus gentium.*

The next issue that presents itself is the origin of spoken language and its relation to the *sensus communis.* But before addressing that issue it will be profitable to summarize how Vico's rhetorical background already controls his account of the imaginative universal.

The Baroque notion of metaphor controls Vico's description of the giants' response to thunder and the creation of the fable of Jove. The imaginative universal is exactly the kind of conceit that Vico called the "brightest ornament" of speech, one that gives life to inanimate bodies. Furthermore, the metaphor is both auditory and visual and generates Jove as a kind of synesthesia. But orality is primary in that it is sound that identifies the sky as alive, and it is sound that provides the opportunity for interpretation. The giants do not, for example, try to "read" Jove's meaning in the movement of the clouds. They respond to the immediacy of sound with bodily fear, which in turn provokes the metaphoric leap.

Another aspect of Vico's theory of metaphor surfaces in his account of the imaginative universal: his claim that metaphors are arguments and can be drawn from the rhetorical topics. The imaginative universal is also a vast enthymeme in that it connects two propositions—sky equals body and thunder equals his voice—by means of a ligamen that implies a conclusion: the sky is God. This metaphor "argues" for certain immediate action: flight into caves, interpretation of the thunder, and subsequent obedience to its directives.

The third influence of rhetoric is the way Vico conceives the mind operating "topically," that is, the way the primary sense experience of the first men is organized into nonverbal *topoi* that provide an index for perceiving and organizing other data. Here Vico remains true to the views he expressed in the *De nostri* that topics must precede criticism, that the mind must first explore and organize information before it can operate critically. Vico posited a mental operation within the first men that was analogous to the use of the topics in inventing a speech, but the first men operated without words and used only sense impressions formed into metaphors.

The final influence of Vico's rhetorical theory is that of the Roman notion of *sententia*. The way the imaginative universal combines sensation with decision is obviously reminiscent of Quintillian's remark about the *sententia* of the Roman courts being related to the verb *sentio*, to feel or sense. The *auctoritas* of the court, and of the law in general, is analogous to the way the mind certifies the data of sensation.

SENSUS COMMUNIS AND THE POETIC LOGIC

In tracing the movement from the fable of the imaginative universal to articulate speech Vico followed the classical writers in positing three ages of man: the golden, the bronze, and the iron, or as he termed them, the divine age, the age of heroes, and the age of men. Each age had a speech proper to it, and more significantly, each had a writing proper to it. Vico held that writing and speech began simultaneously:

> But the difficulty as to the manner of their origin [letters] was created by the scholars themselves, all of whom regarded the origin of letters as a separate question from that of the origin of languages, whereas the two were by nature conjoined. And they should have made out as much from the words "grammar" and "characters." From the

former, because grammar is defined as the art of speaking, yet *grammata* are letters, so that grammar should have been defined as the art of writing. So, indeed, it was defined by Aristotle [*Topics* 142b 31], and so in fact it originally was; for all nations began to speak by writing, since all were originally mute. "Character," on the other hand, means idea, form, model; and certainly poetic characters came before those of articulate sounds [that is, before alphabetic characters]. . . . Thus in their hopeless ignorance of the way in which language and letters began, scholars have failed to understand how the first nations thought in poetic characters, spoke in fables, and wrote in hieroglyphs. *(New Science* 429)[6]

As the quotation indicates, Vico thought that in the first age, the age of gods and of imaginative universals, men spoke in fables (metaphors), which Vico calls *logos* (401), and wrote hieroglyphics (pictures). The age of metaphor is characterized by identity. The second age, the age of heroes, is the age of metonymy, the trope of cause and effect, or the trope that substitutes the container for the contained, as when we say we understand a book when we mean we understand what is in the book. The heroes, says Vico, spoke in symbols, that is, metaphors, images, and other tropes all drawn from sensation, as when, for example, a Homeric hero says "the blood boils in my heart" when he means he is angry (438, 460). But the heroes knew that these were figures, that they were dealing in similarities not identities as the giants did. To notice that the sea is "wine-dark" is also to see that it is not wine. The heroes wrote in what Vico calls *semeia,* signs, or what we should call heraldic symbols, in which objects like lions rampant stand for the anger or bravery of the family or clan. Finally, Vico describes the age of men as an age characterized by synecdoche, the trope that identifies wholes and parts, as when we say "All hands on deck" when we mean all sailors on deck. In this age people speak in abstract terms such as "anger" or "bravery" and write with a phonetic alphabet that reduces sounds to a system of signs common to all articulate words. Finally, the age of men comes to an end when men become possessed by the "barbarism of reflection." The decay in social institutions is matched by a growing solipsism in philosophy. Vico characterizes this decay with the trope of irony. In its last days, a community turns to ironic discourse to recall the consensus it has lost. Even this eventually fails, and men return to the forests, where the cycle repeats itself.

These are the three ages of man, each with its appropriate language and writing. Vico assigns the origins of the languages to certain classes: the language of the divine age with the "theological poets"; the heroic language with the heroes; and the language of men, the "vulgar language," with the *famuli* of the heroes, those family members who shared the heroic language but were eventually given reduced status in the clan; from them the language passed to the plebeians or serfs of the heroes (443). This "vulgar language," Vico says, was implicit in the natural affinities between the two terms of a metaphor that the "theological poets" (those who interpreted the thunder and created the imaginative universals) first noted. For example, there must be something about the top of a hill which resembles a brow, or the identity could not be created at all. This identity became consciously metaphoric in heroic language; the heroes knew that a hill and a brow were *similar* but not identical. Vulgar tongues preserve these metaphors inherited from the heroic language. Vico expressly denies that vernacular language originates with arbitrary signification (444).

We must be careful not to interpret Vico as saying that these stages follow one another exclusively, or that any stage excludes all aspects of the others. There is nothing to indicate that in the age of the heroes men walked about speaking only in tropes or that figurative language is unknown or suppressed in the age of men. A clearer way to understand Vico's ages would be to see them as accounts of how certain communities formulated institutions that can be described in terms of the discourse the community would use unconsciously to create and interpret them. In a heroic culture, the heroes appropriate divinity, or at least access to divinity, to themselves. They contain *arete* or *virtù* or whatever quality defines the hero. At the same time, this distinguishes them from all those who do not contain or embody the heroic quality and perforce allows the heroes to define themselves against those people. Vico is using the figuration usually associated with heroic literature to characterize heroic culture itself. He makes a similar analogy with the age of gods and the age of men. He never suggests that the entire community operates at only one level or that the groups not in control are deprived of their own form of language. Rather, he asserts that the institutions of the community are created and interpreted in terms of the trope proper to that particular stage, but that the others may still exist, and in fact must exist if hegemony is to pass to them.

The question arises of how these stages actually come into being, how they achieve hegemony, and how each passes to another stage. This process Vico calls the "poetic logic." In describing the poetic logic Vico is describing how the imaginative universals permeate language as the *sensus communis* and empower it, give it the ability to change human affairs through eloquence.

Vico first turns his attention to how the original golden age gave way to an age of heroes. His account exemplifies the way he uses etymology to explore the relation between language and social institutions.

> it is not beyond likelihood that, when wonder had been awakened in men by the first thunderbolts, these interjections of Jove should give birth to one produced by the human voice: *pa!;* and that this should then be doubled: *pape!* From this interjection of wonder was subsequently derived Jove's title of father of men and gods, and thus it came about presently that all the gods were called fathers, and the goddesses, mothers. . . . (448)
>
> The strong men in the family state, from a natural ambition of human pride, arrogated to themselves this divine title of fathers . . . but, observing the piety they owed to the deities, they called the latter gods. (449)

Vico continues to apply his etymological method to the history of ancient economics, politics, religion, and morals. In each instance he reveals how the history of a cultural institution can be traced by revealing the primary metaphors operating in a language's more abstract terms. These etymologies are not historically accurate because Vico argues from homonyms. He was, after all, working before the brothers Grimm. But his arguments always lead to the same conclusion: that language, even the abstract language of law and philosophy, is derived from metaphors that reflect the primal, community-founding judgments of the first men.

These metaphors are, of course, the imaginative universals, which served the founders of humanity as a "sensory topics." But after the creation of the "fathers" who found the first families, the heroes gradually appropriate the language and imagery of the divine. The emergence of clans with clients causes the society to develop into more complex social units, the village and the city, and the metaphoric language of the first fathers gives way to the metonymic language of the heroes who appropriate access to divinity to themselves and excludes the nonheroic, the plebs or serfs. Hence the heroes have their own language, and it is the language of the gods, that is, the heroes retain knowledge of the auspices to which the rest of the community is denied access.

Vico's great example of this process is the Roman republic. The patricians denied the plebs access to the auspices. This denial had important consequences, as Vico explains. The plebs could not marry in the eyes of the state because they were not fully admitted to the religion. Because they could not contract civilly valid marriages, they were denied inheritance rights. Because they were denied inheritance rights, their right to own property was severely restricted. This is the sequence of Vico's dialectic: from religion to language, from language to human institutions (institutions that all people practice: religion, marriage, and burial of the dead), from these institutions to property rights, and then to broader legal rights. The entire state of affairs is controlled by the interpenetration of religion, language, and social class. The language of the auspices gives the patricians a religious rationale for denying full citizenship (which meant full humanity) to the plebs. Hence the social condition is characterized by metonymy, the trope of cause and effect, the container (the patricians) for the contained (the auspices and their attendant rights).

The development of the rights of the plebs is Vico's example of the movement from the age of heroes to the age of men, from the age of metonymy to the age of synecdoche. Vico points to the Roman Laws of the Twelve Tables as moving the Roman republic to an age of "men." The plebs desire written laws, says Vico; the patricians oppose them (284). Because the laws are written, the plebs feel assured of consistent treatment, but the enforcement of the written law does not measure up to their expectations. But, because the law is written, the plebs are in a position to claim certain rights they believe inhere in its text. Vico's specific example of this is the second agrarian law granted in the Twelve Tables. This law gave the plebs rights of ownership, but it did not give them rights of inheritance or citizenship. Hence, the lands they "owned" soon returned to the nobles. Vico explains that "What they did ask was the right to contract solemn nuptials just as the fathers did, and so they demanded *connubia patrum,* the principal solemnity of which was the public auspices called by Varro and Messala major auspices, those meant by the fathers when they said the auspices were theirs. The plebeians, in making this demand, were in effect asking for Roman citizenship, whose natural principle was solemn nuptials . . ." (598).

This situation was also subject to abuse and received correction: the establishment of the tribunes, other agrarian reforms, and finally the reform of Fabius Maximus, which divided the Roman people into three classes: senators, knights, and plebeians to be determined by their wealth. In short, the plebeians could become senators if they were rich enough (619). Thus the plebs gained access to the full definition of manhood or citizenship, the part became identified with the whole.

Vico describes how Roman legislation and administration gradually admitted the plebs to the ranks of the patricians by interpreting and reinterpreting the original laws and customs. This process was achieved, first, by writing down the laws, that is, by the invention of what Vico called "vulgar letters," writing to which even the common folk had access as opposed to the *semeia,* which only the heroes could understand. The second factor in such reform was eloquence. Vico pictures these reforms occurring in the drama of public debate on the rostrum, in the forum, and in the senate. Each piece of legislation, each new practice, was debated publicly and argued for in terms of the prior tradition. Here extemporaneous public debate created social institutions by formulating new policy expressed in the language of traditional values.

The modern world is not without examples of what Vico means. The oxymoron "loyal opposition" created the two-party system in England, where previously the opposing party was viewed by the government as treasonous. Likewise, in the Gettysburg Address, Lincoln expanded the meaning of "men" in the phrase "all men are created equal" to include those of the black race, an inclusion that the original framers of the Declaration of Independence certainly did not intend. But Lincoln's redefiniton of "men" to include white males and black males would have been improbable without the popular writings of the abolitionists. *Uncle Tom's Cabin* prepared the way for the Gettysburg Address, but even that work built upon a literary tradition—and a religious one. Today, civil rights movements point out the failures of America to totally integrate blacks into its society, and some women insist that the term *men* in the Declaration and Gettysburg Address excludes them. Thus the effort to use synecdoche to interpret the *sensus communis* continues.

Mere eloquence, of course, cannot achieve reform, but Vico, as I understand him, says that policy reform, institutional reform, or social change is impossible without it. Such change occurs when language reformulates traditional value to express and justify a new constellation of institutional structures. The intersection of language and social structure is achieved by ingenuity, the imaginative leap that finds similarity in two things that are apparently dissimilar, as in "loyal opposition." Such eloquence makes the change understandable; it "makes sense" to the community at large.

Here the *sensus communis* in the legal sense meets *sensus communis* in the rhetorical sense. The language of a community contains within its metaphors and other figures the affective, pre-reflective meaning created in the imaginative universals and perpetuated in the "common sensuality" of the language. The language also contains the values or "prejudices" that have accumulated in the community's choices since their origin in the imaginative universals. The imaginative universals are the *arche* of the two meanings of *sensus communis:* "common sensuality" and "judgment without reflection"; custom, institutions, and eventually law reflect, and are created out of, the primal metaphors imbedded in language, metaphors that unite communal judgment with affective power.

Vico summarizes this unity at the conclusion of Book II of the *New Science:* "And it may be said that in the fables the nations have in a rough way and in the language of the human senses described the beginnings of this world of sciences, which the specialized studies of the scholars have since clarified for us by reasoning and generalization. From all this we may conclude what we set out to show in this Book: that the theological poets were the sense and the philosophers the intellect of human wisdom" (779).

Vico posits the origin of sense in the work of the theological poets, those who first created the imaginative universals and interpreted them, thus forming human community and creating the basis of language. This insight, he says, is available in the fables, and, Vico says, every metaphor is a fable in brief. By uniting emotional force with practical judgment these metaphors find their way into language. Thus the *sensus communis* is available to orators and poets as they deal with new problems and "utilities" permitting them to make the solutions "sensible" to their audience. The "philosophers" are those who developed abstract thought from the sensory topics and who articulated it in abstract, philosophical language. Vico thus claims to have established the unity of poetic and philosophical thought, a unity that humanism traditionally found in rhetoric.

The relation of poetry and philosophy has become the focal point of contemporary criticism, and the following chapters deal with those twentieth-century thinkers whose theories still draw upon the traditions Vico was opposing or adapting, for example, Gadamer's philosophical hermeneutics and Derrida's deconstruction. These two critical schools, in one way or another, adapt or oppose Vico's concept of *sensus communis,* and by investigating how they approach it, we can understand Vico's own theory of rhetoric and its importance.

5 Sensus Communis *in Vico and Gadamer*

Hans Georg Gadamer's *Truth and Method* (1960) has achieved the status of a classic hermeneutical work. It uses the insights of Heideggerian philosophy to challenge the claims to scientific certitude made by the human sciences. Gadamer, following Heidegger, argues that language is involved in everything that human beings do, including science, and there can be no scientific objectivity about human beings and human society because there is no place "outside" language from which human beings can be observed.

In developing his ideas, Gadamer displays immense erudition, tracing the development of the social sciences in German Romanticism and exploring the permutations of hermeneutical theory with regard to the human sciences since the early nineteenth century. In making this historical reconstruction Gadamer continually refers to the sources of interpretive theory in classical and humanistic thought. One of these sources is *sensus communis*. In fact, Gadamer says that Vico's appeal to *sensus communis* belongs "in a wider context that goes right back to antiquity and the continued effect of which into the present day is the subject of our book" *(WM* 1965, 21/*TM* 1975, 23).[1]

Gadamer's handling of *sensus communis* controls his hermeneutics. As Joel Weinsheim points out, Gadamer's real agenda is to make the classics relevant once again (1985, 133), and *sensus communis* is, as we have seen, the way Vico saw the relevance of the classics in the rhetorical tradition. But Gadamer is not working within the rhetorical tradition. Rather, he tries to bring hermeneutics into the Greek philosophical tradition, and he tries to bring *sensus communis* along with it. But *sensus communis* is really too conditioned by the rhetorical tradition to be transferred to another intellectual discipline totally, so Gadamer tries to bring into his hermeneutics those aspects of *sensus communis* he needs, while simultaneously fractioning it into separable parts, destroying the holistic treatment of it which he inherited from Vico. The effect of this division is to render his hermeneutic vulnerable in its approach to truth and in its relevance to society as a whole. First, I will examine how Gadamer limits Vico's idea of *sensus communis* and divides it into constituent parts, and then I will discuss the effects of this procedure on his hermeneutical theory itself.[2]

Gadamer beings by revising the definition of *sensus communis* that Vico gives in the *New Science*. That definition was "Judgment without reflection, shared by an entire class, an entire people, an entire nation, or the entire human race" *(New Science* 142). Gadamer, without averting to the *New Science,* defines *sensus communis* as "the concrete generality that represents the community of a group, a people, a nation, or the whole human race" *(WM* 1965, 18/*TN* 1975, 21). This nearly repeats Vico's definition word for word but substitutes "concrete generality that represents" for "judgment without reflection shared." A few pages later, Gadamer refers to taste, quoting Tetens, as "judicium without reflection" *(WM* 1965, 27/*TM* 1975, 30). Gadamer's change is significant. He has removed judgment from Vico's definition and transferred it to taste, and he proceeds to argue that ethical judgment is analogous to taste. In another passage Gadamer confronts the problem of the epistemology of *sensus communis*. Gadamer contrasts St. Thomas's idea of *sensus communis* with Vico's: "In scholasticism, say St. Thomas in his commentary on the *De Anima,* the sensus communis is the common root of the outer sense, ie the faculty that combines them, that makes judgments about what is given, a faculty that is given to all men. For Vico, however, the sensus communis is the sense of right and the general good that is to be found in all men, moreover, a sense that is acquired through living in the community and is determined by its structures and aims" *(WM* 1965, 19/*TM* 1975, 22).

Once again, Gadamer is restricting Vico's *sensus communis* to an ethical consensus and denying that it is a judging faculty. In this case, he is denying that Vico's concept has any relation to intellectual judgment, the way the mind forms universal concepts based on individual sense perceptions. Gadamer must therefore locate both ethical and intellectual judgment somewhere else. How he does so can be seen by examining both his treatment of Vico and the following two passages. Gadamer cites Vico's *De nostri temporis studiorum ratione* as his source for Vico's thinking on *sensus communis (WM* 1965, 16/*TM* 1975, 19). He distinguishes Vico's *sensus communis* from "common sense": "The main thing for our purposes is that sensus communis here obviously does not mean only that general faculty in all men, but the sense that founds community. According to Vico, what gives the human will its direction is not the abstract generality of reason, but the concrete generality that represents the community of a group, a people, a nation or the whole human race. Hence the development of this sense of the community is of prime importance for living" *(WM* 1965, 18/*TM* 1975, 21). Gadamer then proceeds to relate Vico's *sensus communis* to rhetoric's concern with probability: "On this general sense of the true and the right, which is not a knowledge based on argumentation, but enables one to discover what is obvious (verisimile), Vico bases the significance and the independent rights of rhetoric . . ." (*WM* 1965, 18/*TM* 1975, 21).

Finally, Gadamer cites the ethical component in Vico's idea of *sensus communis:*

> there is a positive ethical element involved that passes into the Roman Stoic teaching about sensus communis. The grasp and moral control of the concrete situation require this subsumption of what is given under the universal; ie the goal that one is pursuing so that the right thing may result. Hence it assumes a direction of the will, ie moral being (hexis). That is why Aristotle considers phronesis as an "intellectual virtue." He sees it . . . as a determination of moral being. . . . The distinction between what should and should not be done includes the distinction between the proper and the improper and thus presumes a moral attitude which it continues to develop. (*WM* 1965, 19/*TN* 1975, 21–22).

In these passages Gadamer rightly argues that *sensus communis* for Vico is derived from the rhetorical tradition, that it is similar to Aristotle's *phronesis;* it is a practical knowledge with ethical dimensions and, most important, its use as an ethical norm presumes that it already exists within the moral attitude of an acting subject.

First, as we have seen, Gadamer denies that Vico's idea of *sensus communis* has any relation to the Aristotelian concept of *sensus communis* as the faculty that judges concerning universals. Gadamer sees where

Vico's definition of *sensus communis* can lead: "This idea sounds related to the natural law, like the koinai ennoiai of the stoics" *(WM* 1965, 19/*TM* 1975, 22). But Gadamer refuses to explore the relation of *sensus communis* to natural law because

> sensus communis is not, in this sense a Greek idea and definitely does not mean the koine dunamis of which Aristotle speaks in the *De Anima,* when he seeks to reconcile the doctrine of the specific senses (aisthesis idia) with the phenomenological finding that shows all perception to be a differentiation and an intention of the universal. Rather Vico goes back to the old Roman idea of the sensus communis, as found especially in the Roman classics which, when faced with Greek cultivation, held firmly to the value and significance of their own traditions of public and social life. *(WM* 1965, 19/*TM* 1975, 22)

Gadamer does not see any relation between the Roman idea of *sensus communis* and the Greek meaning of *sensus communis.* The former is an ethical concept related to natural law, the latter an epistemological concept related to the problem of universals. Gadamer wants the rhetorical meaning of *sensus communis,* but without any connotation of judgment.

After having distinguished the Aristotelian idea of *sensus communis* from ethical and intellectual judgment, as well as from Vico's idea, Gadamer introduces the idea of *sensus communis* developed by Shaftesbury. Gadamer is interested in how Shaftesbury sees *sensus communis* operating within the individual: "It is not so much as a feature given to all men, part of the natural law, as a social virtue, a virtue of the heart more than the head, that Shaftesbury is thinking of" *(WM* 1965, 22/*TM* 1975, 24).

Gadamer, moving away from Vico's meaning, with its implied connection to natural law, locates *sensus communis* in "the heart." He proceeds to link Shaftesbury's idea of *sensus communis* with Shaftesbury's idea of taste to show how the *sensus communis* assists taste in making moral judgments as well as aesthetic ones:

> Nor can the meaning of sensus communis be limited merely to aesthetic judgment. From the use that Vico and Shaftesbury make of this idea, it appears that sensus communis is not primarily a

formal capacity, an intellectual faculty that has to be used but already embraces a sum of judgments and judgmental criteria that determine its contents.

Common sense is seen primarily in the judgments about right and wrong, proper and improper, that it makes. *(WM* 1965, 28–29/ *TM* 1975, 30–31)

First Gadamer says that *sensus communis* is not an intellectual capacity, then he says that it is seen in the judgments it makes. If it is not a capacity or faculty, how can it make judgments? The only way this passage can make sense is to understand *sensus communis* as a criterion. *Sensus communis* somehow incorporates certain community values that inform the judging faculty, but it is not the faculty itself.

When Gadamer bases ethical judgment on Shaftesbury's idea of taste, he argues that aesthetic and ethical judgments are made in an analogous way, and he describes this judgment as "without reflection," as noted previously. This unreflective judgment, however, is only a faculty of the individual, not, as it was for Vico, also a possession of the community. To this extent Gadamer has "individualized" Vico's "judgment without reflection," moved it under the rubric of taste and used Shaftesbury's idea of *sensus communis* to smooth the transition.

Thus Gadamer discusses three separate meanings of *sensus communis:* Vico's, which he cites as the general sense of the community; Aristotle's and St. Thomas's, which is the sense that coordinates and distinguishes the perceptions of the other senses to arrive at universal concepts; and Shaftesbury's, which is an emotional, subjective quality that informs taste, and taste, in turn, makes the individual judgment on nondiscursive grounds.

SENSUS COMMUNIS AND NATURAL LAW
IN VICO AND GADAMER

In the *De nostri temporis studiorum ratione* (which Gadamer cites as his source for Vico's views on *sensus communis),* Vico, as we have seen, develops *sensus communis* as a norm for both moral and aesthetic judgment at both the individual and community levels. As Vico says, "common sense, besides being the standard of practical judgment, is also the guiding standard of eloquence" *(De nostri* 13). Vico combines aesthetic judgment and moral consensus under the rubric of *sensus communis,* whereas Gadamer separates judgment from *sensus communis* and substitutes Shaftesbury's notion of taste. Later, in the *New Science,* Vico develops a theory to explain how eloquence draws upon the moral consensus of the community to form judgments about needs and utilities. This moral consensus is common to all human communities, and in the *New Science* Vico draws a conclusion from this commonality: "This axiom is a great principle which establishes the common sense of the human race as the criterion taught to the nations by divine providence to define what is certain in the natural law of the gentes. And the nations reach this certainty by recognizing the underlying agreements which despite variations of detail obtain among them all in respect of this law" (145).

Vico specifically makes the connection between *sensus communis* and the "natural law of the gentes" that Gadamer did not make. *Sensus communis* provides a criterion that certifies communal decisions by recognizing the "underlying agreements" that obtain within the community. These "underlying agreements" are the unreflective judgments that incorporate the natural law in a given community. Vico claims that from these underlying agreements issues "the mental dictionary for assigning origins to all the diverse articulated languages" (145). The unreflective judgments about needs and utilities form the substratum that underlies all human language, relates language to the "law of the gentes," and is brought to consciousness in public discourse.

What, in the *De nostri,* was a relationship between the individual imagination of an orator and the language and tradition of his audience now becomes a dialectic between shared values and shared language acting on both communal and universal levels. Thus *sensus communis* becomes the "public ground of truth"—the ground of the relationship between judgment and language, a ground inhabited by both the individual and the community.

At this point we can see how Vico addressed the issue Gadamer leaves to St. Thomas: the epistemological status of *sensus communis.* Although Gadamer agrees with Vico that *sensus communis,* conceived as a "moral sense of the community," is a given, and that it is given in language, Gadamer did not relate that meaning to the meaning of *sensus communis* as intellectual judgment. But Vico does, and in doing so he conceptualizes just how *sensus communis,* as a shared ethical sense, can be related to the formation of universal concepts.

The imaginative universals synthesize the idea of *sensus communis* as an organizing sense, one that makes sense out of the stimuli received by the other senses, and *sensus communis* conceived as a shared moral sense that exists and develops historically. The imaginative universals organize sense perceptions into images laden with communal value. They become the basis for ancient poetry as well as ancient law and tradition.

The *sensus communis* is exemplified in Vico's thought by the Laws of the Twelve Tables and what he called in the *New Science* "the true Homer" (780–914). He argues that Homer was the Greek people. In other words, Homer's poetry represents the collective, common wisdom of the Greek people, a wisdom that embodied the "law of the gentes," and his poetry kept that wisdom current in Greek thought and society by providing the Greeks with a shared linguistic heritage. Likewise, the Laws of the Twelve Tables provided Roman society with a consensus of law and custom that provided both continuity to social development and a touchstone for legal interpretation of language.[3] For Vico, these texts provided the living synthesis of moral judgment with the apprehension of sense data, that is, their language combined the natural law and pre-reflective meaning. This synthesis was available in the study of rhetoric. Indeed, the synthesis was expressed by Quintillian in the concept of the *sententia.* But the Roman synthesis of sense data, aesthetic judgment, and moral consensus also included a concept of natural law, 'a concept inimical to the Greek philosophical tradition to which Gadamer wants to reshape *sensus communis.*

To adapt *sensus communis* to the Greek philosophical tradition Gadamer divides its content (moral consensus) and its form (aesthetic beauty) from its function, judgment. In the Roman tradition, and in Vico, these three are united in effective oral performance. Having used Shaftesbury and Aristotle to justify these distinctions, Gadamer proceeds to generate an account of how moral consensus functions, an account that attempts to include the classics and authority, but include them by allowing them to participate in his model of hermeneutics.

VICO'S *SENSUS COMMUNIS* AND
GADAMER'S "PREJUDICE"

Despite their allegiance to differing traditions, rhetoric, and philosophy, many of Vico's and Gadamer's insights are similar. Both use jurisprudence as a model for interpretation and judgment; both feature the canon of classical literature as the vehicle for transmitting literary tradition; both feature orality over writing as the premier way in which literary tradition is handed on. Yet behind these evident similarities lies one major difference that complicates the attempt to bring Gadamer and Vico into dialogue. Vico reconstructed the origins of *sensus communis* in oral performance. Gadamer, on the other hand, sees *sensus communis* as the origin of something else, the emergence of literate critical thinking from philosophical challenges to it.

Gadamer does not use the term *sensus communis* except in Vico's and Shaftesbury's sense. When he wishes to speak of the inherited values and images out of which a culture or its texts emerge he refers to "tradition" and "prejudice." Gadamer begins his treatment of prejudice precisely where Vico began his treatment of *sensus communis:* with a critique of the Enlightenment. "And there is one prejudice of the Enlightenment that is essential to it: the fundamental prejudice of the Enlightenment is the prejudice against prejudice itself, which deprives tradition of its power" (*WM* 1965, 255/*TM* 1975, 239–240).

Gadamer wishes to establish prejudice, and tradition which is a whole network of prejudices, as preexisting and predetermining rational judgment, thus undermining the claims to complete objectivity made on behalf of Rationalistic methodologies. "Long before we understand ourselves through the process of self-examination, we understand ourselves in a self-evident way in the family, society and the state in which we live . . . the prejudices of the individual, far more than his judgments, constitute the historical reality of his being" (*WM* 1965, 261/*TM* 1975, 245).

Gadamer states clearly that people acquire their prejudices, at least in part, from authority exercised in the family and by society and the state, primarily in the form of education. This authority is legitimated by the person who exercises it. The individual who is being taught is not in a position to judge the authority, rather he or she accepts what the authority says because of the person who has the authority (*WM* 1965, 263–64/*TM* 1975, 249).

Gadamer pursues the locus of prejudice no further. He is only concerned with demonstrating that prejudice is inescapable and that it is a necessary condition for truth. In short, he is asserting, contrary to Descartes, that a prejudice can be true, and that the only issue is to identify a prejudice as such and then see whether or not it is true. Furthermore, he is asserting, contrary to Wilhelm Dilthey, that the starting point of any inquiry is historically conditioned and not an ahistorical intuition.

Because a prejudice is an inherited value, one that predisposes one to certain judgments of right and wrong, it would be easy to identify it with Vico's *sensus communis*. However, Gadamer himself does not so identify it, and in fact he says *sensus communis* "embraces a sum of judgments and judgmental criteria which determine its content" *(WM* 1965, 29/*TM* 1975, 31). Hence prejudice is not *sensus communis,* but rather prejudices make up *sensus communis*'s "content." Furthermore, as we have seen, for Vico *sensus communis* inheres in language and allows communities to form institutions according to the dictates of the natural law. Those institutions include the family, society, and eventually, the state. For Gadamer, on the other hand, these institutions inculcate prejudices, which in turn form the *sensus communis.* The difference is crucial. What Gadamer sees as the origin of *sensus communis,* that is, institutions, Vico sees as emerging with *sensus communis* along with the imaginative universals. The imaginative universals and institutions come into being at the same time, created by the imagination that perceives similarities and interprets them.

For Vico, the imaginative universals embody the *sensus communis,* and they, in turn, are available in the works of the literary classics that form the content of rhetorical study. In short, for Vico the *sensus communis* is in the classical because the latter is historical. Gadamer, on the other hand, proceeds to hew out a transhistorical locus for the concept of the classic.

A classic is, according to Gadamer, a work that brings to us the sources of our tradition and bridges the gap between its time and ours, showing us the enduring validity of the insights of the past and thus working to constitute the present. This means that "Our understanding [of the classic] will always include our consciousness of belonging to that world" *(WM* 1965, 274/*TM* 1975, 258).

Gadamer explains that "classical" qualifies the usual meaning of "historical": "The Classical is what resists historical criticism because its historical dominion, the binding power of its validity that is preserved and handed down, precedes all historical reflection and continues through it" *(WM* 1965, 271/*TM* 1975, 255). The classical, in short, is what cannot be explained by being placed in a historical perspective. What is perhaps more significant about Gadamer's treatment of the classical is that he isolates its relevance to the individual. When he says "we" belong to its world, the "we" is a community of cultured readers. For Vico, on the contrary, the classics were permanently relevant to society as a whole. They provided the permanent fund of a consensus of human meaning and value that was made available in rhetorical training for making communal decisions, in "making sense" out of new conditions and problems in the realm of "needs and utilities."

Gadamer is aware that tradition is linguistic and that language exists primarily as oral, but, at the same time, he realizes that the locus of such tradition is in the classics and they exist as printed books. He admits the problem: "In writing, language is detached from its full realisation" *(WM* 1965, 367/*TM* 1975, 351), an idea similar to the way Plato himself thought of writing. Gadamer proceeds to defend reading and writing against Plato's attack by showing that it is only within a written tradition that hermeneutic consciousness fully develops.

Gadamer argues that "In writing, language gains its true intellectual quality, for when confronted with a written tradition understanding consciousness acquires its full sovereignty" *(WM* 1965, 368/*TM* 1975, 352). The issue then is how the classics are to be both read and heard. In a virtuoso display of turning his opponent's arguments against him, Gadamer suggests that hermeneutics should be modeled on the Socratic dialogue. The interpreter should regard the text as a "spokesperson" for tradition, one to whom he or she must listen and address questions. Reading the classics, or any text, becomes a process analogous to the Socratic dialogue that Plato wrote. "It is not this document, as coming from the past, that is the bearer of tradition, but the continuity of memory. Through memory tradition becomes part of our own world, and so what it communicates can be directly expressed. Where we have a written tradition, we are not just told an individual thing, but a past humanity itself becomes present to us, in its general relation to the world" (*WM* 1965, 368/*TM* 1975, 352).

Gadamer qualifies the rhetorical, humanistic approach to hermeneutics to include a style of reading modeled on Greek philosophy. He begins his analysis of the hermeneutic experience by describing understanding in terms congenial to the Greek philosophical tradition and antithetical to Dilthey and the German Romantic tradition: "To understand what a person says . . . is to agree about the object, not to get inside the other person and relive his experiences" (*WM* 1965, 361/ TM 1975, 345).

Gadamer makes the operation of tradition analogous to dialogue, that is, he conceives tradition as a "Thou" which speaks to us (*WM* 1965, 340/*TM* 1975, 321). This is an important concept because, if tradition is treated as a person, it cannot be objectified; it cannot be treated as an object itself, that is, the interpreter will confront the text as speaking to him or her with the voice of a tradition. The author is not the "Thou"; the tradition is. And finally, since tradition is personal, Gadamer concludes that encountering it is a moral experience (*WM* 1965, 340/*TM* 1975, 321). Thus the act of understanding a text, which constitutes hermeneutics, is construed along the model of Socratic dialogue: a personal exchange between committed individuals with the goal of challenging received opinion in order to generate new insights that carry moral and ethical force (*WM* 1965, 344–60/*TM* 1975, 325–41).

The issue that must be raised is whether the Greek philosophical tradition and its dialectical method *can* be unified with the traditional, rhetorical understanding of hermeneutics. After all, these two traditions generally saw themselves as opposed to each other. Plato's antagonists were the Sophists, teachers of rhetoric; and Cicero, the greatest of the Roman orators, said that Socrates had ruined philosophy.

Vico and Gadamer differ on the status of orality. For Vico, orality is the condition in which the classics exist and in which they are used, that is, the tradition of oral performance controls how he conceives the classics being applied. Gadamer, on the other hand, uses orality as a metaphor for the interaction of text and reader, that is, the orality of dialogue, but the tradition in which the texts actually exist is the rhetorical tradition. By trying to impart a rhetorically based idea of tradition and *phronesis* into a dialogic model of reading, Gadamer has conflated rhetorical and philosophical ideas of truth. Second, by excluding *phronesis* and judgment from *sensus communis,* he appears to have doomed his hermeneutic to social impotence. By investigating these problems in turn, we shall see the implications of Gadamer's diminished sense of orality as contrasted with Vico's properly oral concept of *sensus communis.*

VICO AND GADAMER ON TRUTH

Gadamer's theory of truth has been challenged by many critics, especially by Richard Bernstein, Georgia Warnke, and Lawrence Hinman. Hinman points out that Gadamer claims only to be describing what in fact occurs when an interpreter grasps a truth (1980). Gadamer disavows any attempt to prescribe what should happen in a hermeneutical situation. What in fact does happen is a grasping of truth that is bound to tradition and within tradition. Hinman argues that Gadamer's account of understanding is, as it were, "generic," that is, he describes understanding in general, but does not allow one to ascertain if any one particular case of interpretation results in a grasping of truth (1980, 532). Bernstein raises a similar objection when he says that Gadamer seems to imply that truth is discovered by argument but provides no criteria by which to validate arguments about ideas such as tradition or authority: "It is not *sufficient* to give a justification that directs us to tradition. What is required is a form of argumentation that seeks to warrant what is valid in this tradition" (1983, 155).

Georgia Warnke questions whether Gadamer's hermeneutics ever break out of a purely subjective idea of truth. She argues that the well-known "hermeneutic circle" is actually a vicious circle, that an interpreter who goes from the part to the whole of a work, or from the whole to a part, can never escape the prejudices and traditions which are also part of his or her own view, but must interpret them too. In other words, the prejudices and traditions are also the object of a hermeneutic circle, and so on ad infinitum (1987, 75–91).

Hinman and Bernstein point out the difficulty Gadamer has in adapting rhetorically controlled ideas like tradition, authority, and the classical to a dialectical model of hermeneutics. If these ideas are taken as controlling the situation in which truth can be grasped, and hermeneutics is taken as the dialectical interrogation of them, then the truth that is discovered is always the truth of tradition itself. If hermeneutics describes only what in fact occurs, what difference does knowing about it make? What kind of truth is revealed?

As Eric Havelock has pointed out, the idea of truth Plato develops is one that depends upon the interiorization of literacy (1963). For Plato, truth means an insight into the generic, the "form" of a thing, and this kind of abstraction is only possible when one conceives language as separable from things. This sort of truth is arrived at by interrogating meaning, by asking what a word means to someone, a question that a non-literate person could formulate only with great difficulty if at all. Truth then becomes a new meaning, grasped as a result of mutual interrogation of an already given, unsatisfactory meaning. In a certain sense, then, it is correct to say that for Plato, truth is always truth against something.

The Greek philosophical tradition attempted to qualify, if not eradicate, certain aspects of oral culture, aspects that have been described by Walter Ong (1982, 31–71). Those aspects would have included an inability to dissociate value from image (hence the Platonic prohibition on poetry), an inability to think abstractly, and a complete dependence on oral tradition and proverb lore as a basis for practical judgment. Socrates' method, later dramatized by Plato in written form, was to challenge the inherited, unreflective values of oral tradition by asking his interlocutors questions about the meaning of words. This questioning brought the moral consensus into consciousness, and, regardless of the answers, the process itself made the individual more reflective. This process requires that meaning and word be mentally separable, that they are perceived as reified outside of a specific context. But, unlike Socrates and Plato, Gadamer is trying to apply this method to people who are already literate. One of the central issues here is whether tradition and its prejudices are like Vico's *sensus communis* or like the *doxa,* the common opinion, which Socrates and Plato wanted to challenge—or like neither one.

One way to see this problem is to consider the sort of good upon which the *sensus communis* was established. Aristotle called the ability to determine the good in practical situations and to use practical judgment to achieve the good, *phronesis*. Gadamer carefully points out that Aristotle developed his idea of *phronesis* in contradistinction to Plato's "idea of the good" *(WM* 1965, 18–19/*TM* 1975, 22). It is *phronesis,* Gadamer says, which forms the background of Vico's idea of *sensus communis* and not the *koinai dunamis,* the common sense of which St. Thomas speaks. The point is well taken, but it leaves Gadamer the problem of trying to make a rhetorically controlled notion of *sensus communis* the basis of an interpretive procedure conceived along a Socratic model.

The issue here is not merely one of sources. Rather, it concerns one of the oldest and most important problems of Western civilization: the status of the idea of the good in philosophy as opposed to its status in rhetoric. Vico's *sensus communis* means the community's sense of what is good. That good is easily equated with precisely those "opinions" *(doxa)* against which Socrates and Plato directed their dialectic. For Plato, *doxa* was never the truth because it was never interiorized individually but always held as an unreflective, orally based communal possession. Gadamer tries to translate this notion of *doxa* into written tradition; the classical text speaks tradition, and the reader is supposed to interrogate both text and self, deciding if the prejudices the reader and it hold are true. This process differs radically from the Platonic dialogue that pits the literate reader against oral tradition. Gadamer pits text and tradition against reader.

Greek dialectic, Gadamer's hermeneutic model, infers a concept of truth drawn from Platonism, yet, as Bernstein points out, Gadamer actually wants the hermeneutic process to yield *phronesis* (1983, 40). Gadamer wants Aristotelian truth from Socratic dialogue, or, put another way, by describing the reading process as dialogic, he argues that it will yield practical truth about tradition yet within tradition.

Vico's idea of *sensus communis* exfoliates the interrelation of tradition, history, and the classical in another way, one that presumes a concept of truth different from that of Greek philosophy. Vico's concept is derived from the tradition of Roman rhetoric. Rather than clarifying meaning for an individual by a process of introspection that distinguishes meaning from oral tradition, rhetoric discovers truth by using training in literacy to apply tradition to praxis. Dialectic seeks to define meaning; rhetoric to refine it, to make it more precise within eloquent performance so that certain actions will be taken. Truth, within the rhetorical tradition, is never far from praxis. Briefly recalling Vico's idea of truth will show its potential for resolving some of the difficulties to which a dialectically based hermeneutics must lead, and it will prepare us to investigate Vico's relevance to the *Hermeneutikstreit,* the intense debate about how Gadamer's hermeneutics can ever have any social relevance.

Vico's idea of truth is expressed in his well-known concept of *verum-certum.* That which is *verum,* true, is that which the human mind can know *ab origine* because the human mind can construct it itself. What is outside the mind can only be known as certain *(certum)* because the mind can only know it as an object. Physical nature can never be grasped as "true" because its structure and origin lie outside the human mind. Only God, who created nature, can know it truly.

Vico describes the way the human mind created human society in his account of the imaginative universals. These images are "made true" because the social reality they reflect is called into being precisely when the imaginative universals themselves are created. These imaginative universals are "true" because they reflect the situation that created them. For Vico, the imaginative universals, not prejudice, form the content of the *sensus communis.*

For Gadamer, tradition, and the prejudices of which it is composed, is revised by a dialectical interaction with texts, especially classical texts. For Vico, on the other hand, the *sensus communis* is revised by social action under the influence of eloquence. It is not dialectic that challenges, but imagination that reconstellates, *sensus communis.* What then about the status of the classic? Within the rhetorical tradition, the classic has its value because it provides access to *sensus communis* and the familiar images with which it is expressed. Within the rhetorical tradition, the classic is for training. It is dissected, memorized, and incorporated into the speech and thought habits of the student. For dialectic, the classic is to be challenged, to be argued against. Dialectic sees the classic's historicity as disabling, making the work open to question. For rhetoric, the historicity of the text is a guarantee of its relevance that ensures the continuity of the culture.

Rhetoric and dialectic regard authority differently, too. In the rhetorical tradition, authority is derived from tradition as much as tradition is derived from authority. The teacher of rhetoric, or of grammar for that matter, impersonates the tradition he or she is teaching, and teaches the students to impersonate it too. That is the purpose of so many imitative drills. The dialectician, on the other hand, sets up against tradition. His or her students, too, are supposed to adopt a critical, not an imitative, attitude toward tradition. The dialectician is not an authority on content, but on form. Like Socrates, he or she impersonates one who does not know so that truth can be discovered, whereas the rhetorician impersonates tradition so that truth can be transmitted.

Vico and Gadamer differ on how truth is tested and how one gains access to it. For Vico, the truth of a classic is a truth one uses in the public arena. It is a *communal* truth. One does not "test" its truth so much as use it to win the assent of others in public discourse. The test of eloquence, for Vico, is *inventio* discovering which truths, which parts of the *sensus communis,* apply to a particular case. When an orator is persuasive, when his arguments sway an audience, he has demonstrated that his arguments actually participate in the *sensus communis* and provide access to it and the imaginative universals that constitute it. Of course, an opponent presumably could appeal to the same *sensus communis* with his arguments. Arguments are adjudicated by an audience. Vico's frequent references to jurisprudence as a creative, imaginative activity testify to his belief that eloquence applies the *sensus communis* to ad hoc, concrete situations, but within the context of adversative public oral performance.

The hurly-burly of oral debate not only applies the *sensus communis* to concrete problems, but also tests and reshapes the *sensus communis* itself. The *sensus communis* cannot be merely a static set of values embodied in a literary canon. Although rhetoric depends heavily upon a consensus of values, that capital to which Richard Weaver referred, it is a capital constantly changing its outline as it is invested in various causes. The *sensus communis* is constantly reinterpreted and reshaped by the decisions of the community. Vico conceives of these decisions as constituting a kind of jurisprudence, a kind of developing interpretive context with which the values contained in classical texts meet the problems of daily life. In short, rhetoric transmits the *sensus communis;* eloquence transmutes it; the community tests it.

Gadamer and Vico also differ radically on the question of access. Gadamer obviously conceives of the dialogue with the classical text as occurring within a silent reading. Vico, on the other hand, thought of the classic as existing within a tradition of oral performance. Rhetoric students performed the texts, recited them from memory, imitated them in both speech and writing. Gadamer is not unaware of the oral matrix of classical literature: "the primacy of hearing is the basis of the hermeneutical phenomenon," because in hearing "language opens up a completely new dimension, the profound dimension whence tradition now comes down to those now living" *(WM* 1965, 438/*TM* 1975, 420). Gadamer, however, does not see any qualitative difference between reading and hearing: "This has always been the true essence of hearing, even before the invention of writing, that the hearer may listen to the legends, the myths and the truth of the ancients. The literary transmission of tradition, as we know it, is nothing new, compared with this, but only changes the form and makes the task of real hearing more difficult" *(WM* 1965, 438/*TM* 1975, 420). "Real hearing" is precisely the issue, because within the humanist matrix of hermeneutics, that hearing occurs within a rhetorical, not a dialogical, situation. Although it may be true that the historical situation of a text cannot totally control its interpretation, the fact remains that certain rhetorical considerations did, in fact, control most classical texts, and, more important, the tradition within which those texts were preserved was the tradition of rhetoric. In other words, rhetoric not only produced those texts, but rhetoric also provided the matrix for their *re*production and interpretation. Rhetoric is the tradition in which classical texts speak tradition.

The orality of the rhetorical tradition, as we have seen, was the ground of Vico's *sensus communis*. To participate in that sense the text must be conceived as existing within certain rhetorical limits and having certain rhetorical characteristics. For Gadamer, the text speaks the tradition orally, but for Vico, the tradition is oral; the text is inserted into a pedagogic, performative tradition rather than into a dialectical philosophical one.

Gadamer describes how a classic text should be read in his section on "application." By this he means that an interpreter must always apply the text he is working on to himself. The text must be fruitful in its interpreter's present situation; the situation in which the text originated is of secondary importance. Application also implies an awareness of the prejudices and the tradition in which the reader finds himself and which have served to form his consciousness. "Application" then means the reader's ability to change his views, to judge his prejudices and his tradition in the light of the text. "The interpreter dealing with a traditional text seeks to apply it to himself . . . the interpreter seeks no more than to understand this universal thing, the text, ie., to understand what this piece of tradition says, what constitutes the meaning and importance of the text. In order to understand that, he must not seek to disregard himself and his particular hermeneutical situation. He must relate the text to this situation, if he wants to understand at all" *(WM* 1965, 307/*TM* 1975, 289). Here Gadamer makes the reader's situation the key to interpretation, not the speaker's situation, which was the focus of rhetoric. Gadamer reiterates this view in *"Rhetorik, Hermeneutik und Ideologiekritik"* (Bleicher 1980, 65).

To recapitulate, Gadamer consistently tries to bring the classic and its tradition into a hermeneutic transaction that imports dialectic into reading. This attempt does violence to the classic's own tradition: rhetoric. Rhetoric is a kind of para-tradition, an academic discipline that preserved classical texts by incorporating them within rigorous training in oral performance. The tradition of rhetoric was an alternative tradition, different from—and to a certain extent, opposed to—the Greek philosophic tradition. It had its own concept of truth and had for its purpose an active life in the community. Thus Gadamer imports into his hermeneutics a conflict between rhetorical, orally based truth, and philosophical, literacy based truth. The former is performative, public, and practical; the latter is private, individual, and theoretical. The reader can only apply what he reads to himself; Gadamer makes no provision for any sort of social action stemming from his hermeneutical theory, and this leads to the second major challenge to that theory: the attack made by members of the Frankfurt School, chiefly Jürgen Habermas, that Gadamer's hermeneutic is powerless to change tradition and is thus an apologetic for the status quo.

SENSUS COMMUNIS AND IDEOLOGY

The *Hermeneutikstreit* between Gadamer and Habermas has produced an immense secondary literature of its own, but it dates from Habermas's publication of his *Erkenntnis und Interesse* in which he attacks Gadamer's *Wahrheit und Methode*. Gadamer responded in an essay entitled *"Rhetorik, Hermeneutik und Ideologiekritik: Metakritische Erörterungen zu Wahrheit und Methode"* (1971), and Habermas responded to that with an essay entitled "The Hermeneutic Claim to Universality" (1980), to which Gadamer responded again. And so on.

The focus of the disagreement is the role of language in Gadamer's hermeneutics, a role Habermas says makes Gadamer's theory impotent really to affect social reality. Gadamer states explicitly that he wishes to undercut the claim of the human sciences to scientific knowledge about the human. The universality of language not only precludes objectivity about the human, but also insures that all understanding must begin with some sort of given "fore-structure" or "fore-understanding," which even determines the sorts of questions that must be asked. Hence language is a universal medium of understanding whose constituent prejudices can be challenged, but only from within.

Habermas points out that this "universality" of language precludes any critique of the social structure which language and ideology sanction. Habermas places himself directly in the Enlightenment tradition Gadamer rejects, and Habermas specifically rejects Gadamer's dialogic model of hermeneutics, quoting A. Wellmer's *Critical Theory of Society:* "The Enlightenment knew what a philosophical hermeneutic forgets—that the 'dialogue' which we, according to Gadamer, 'are' is also a context of domination and as such precisely no dialogue. . . . The universal claim of the hermeneutic approach [can only] be maintained if it is realized at the outset that the context of tradition as a locus of possible truth and factual agreement is, at the same time, the locus of factual untruth and continued force" (Bleicher 1980, 204–5).

Habermas argues passionately that the Enlightenment concept of reason provides leverage to straighten the distortion imbedded in language, distortion that disguises the abuse of power upon which capitalist society rests: "A critically enlightened hermeneutic that differentiates between insight and delusion incorporates the metahermeneutic awareness of the conditions for the possibility of systematically distorted communication. It connects the process of understanding to the principle of rational discourse, according to which truth would only be guaranteed by *that* kind of consensus which was achieved under the idealized conditions of unlimited communication free from domination and could be maintained over time" (Bleicher 1980, 205).

Habermas continues to assert his Enlightenment "prejudice against prejudice." He believes authority to be opposed to reason without qualification (Bleicher 1980, 208), and he rejects tradition as a conveyor of truth until and unless "freedom from force and unrestricted agreement about tradition have already been secured within this tradition" (207). In short, Habermas maintains that dialogue, as Gadamer describes it, occurs within a tradition based on force, and the dialogue helps maintain that tradition, not challenge it.

That dialogue, he concludes, is not possible in the present, but only in an "enlightened" future that a hermeneutics must envision. This specifically contradicts Gadamer's claim that in *Truth and Method* he was only describing how interpretation actually happens. For Habermas, critical interpretation must always look away from what *is* in order to bring about the conditions in which interpretation should occur.

Gadamer responds to Habermas by pointing out that understanding is an existential not methodological act. As such it occurs within a community, not within some sort of patient-client relationship in which the former possesses a critical "method" that leads to enlightenment. On the contrary, the dialogue must occur within a community of dialogue from which nothing can be excluded. Gadamer refers to this dialogue as "the universal medium of practical Reason (and Unreason)" (Bleicher 1980, 157).

Habermas's critique of Gadamer's hermeneutics draws its strength, first, from the way Gadamer bases that hermeneutic on the isolated reader and, second, from his concept of truth that is divorced from the public world. As we have seen, both of these positions result from Gadamer's divorcing of *sensus communis* from practical judgment in order to bring the rhetorically grounded concept of *sensus communis* into the tradition of Greek dialectic. Gadamer's concepts of tradition, prejudice, application, and effective-history fragmented the rhetorical notion of *sensus communis* in order to free it for incorporation into dialectic. But to make it susceptible to criticism by dialectic, he also leaves the notion impotent for all but the private reader.

These changes in Vico's concept of *sensus communis* leave Gadamer with a concept of tradition akin to Greek *doxa* and Marx's ideology, as Habermas is quick to point out. But Vico's *sensus communis* lies far deeper than either Gadamer's idea of an ethical tradition or Habermas's "false consciousness engineered by dominant interests" (Bleicher 1980, 160).

It may be useful to digress about the meaning of community in the thought of Vico, Gadamer, and Habermas. Vico's idea of community is always the civic community and the language community. His conception is political as well as cultural. Furthermore, Vico concerns himself with the *arche* of the community, its language, and institutions. He sees that *arche* in religion prompted by fear and resulting in dominance. Third, his conception is also, like so many other of his concepts, oral, or in this case, auditory. The community is a community of listeners. Finally, the community is potentially all-inclusive. The speaker may possess an elite learning; he may even speak a prestige language, like Latin, but rhetoric itself includes no theoretical limitations on the audience. The more people know about their traditions, the better the speaker's chances for success.

Gadamer's idea of community is purely linguistic and cultural, not political. While the traditions of the community inhere in its institutions and language, Gadamer says nothing about its (or their) *arche*. Gadamer's community of interpreters is differentiated from the larger community. The former are readers who criticize and judge the traditions of the latter.

Habermas regards the community sociologically, as established by power and dominance, an *arche* he shares with Vico, but he dismisses any belief in the efficacy of political action. The community is essentially flawed by ideology and the dominance it justifies. Hence, Habermas insists that genuine community can only exist as an ideal, a future. Finally, those privy to the methods of a Marxist criticism modeled on psychoanalysis have the mission to enlighten the masses, to raise their consciousness to a perception of the ideology that oppresses them and with which they have colluded.

Because Vico's *sensus communis* takes it for granted that communities are communities of dominance and fear, he can articulate a theory of social change that takes account of the social interaction of language and institutions, something Habermas says Gadamer's hermeneutics cannot do. *Sensus communis* allows the poetic logic to operate through eloquence, and thus provides a theory of social change that is an alternative to Cartesian models of rationality or Marxist models of dialectic. Whether Vico's poetic logic actually operates in the sequences he describes is less important than the fact that the poetic logic shows how eloquence can address tradition (*sensus communis*) in the public sphere to effect social change. Thus Vico's *sensus communis* allows for social change when tradition is applied to social realities, whereas Gadamer's notion of tradition allows only for personal change when tradition is applied to, or challenged by, oneself.

The orality implicit in Vico's idea of *sensus communis* allows for a holistic view of tradition, hermeneutic, and social change. Both Gadamer and Habermas opt for a conceptual division between tradition and hermeneutics on the one hand, and social institutions on the other. Their disagreement is over the accessibility of the first two to the latter, or rather, over whether there ought to be accessibility to social institutions. Vico's account of the relation of *sensus communis* to social change exploits the holism implicit in the tradition of oral rhetoric. The young orator incorporates tradition in the oral performance of classical literature, a kind of public *copia* to which the educated have access and their audience understands. Its values and images are exploited as resources to invent and justify social change that is effected by public speaking in the public domain. The rhetorical tradition, as Vico understands it, is a kind of public hermeneutics that is constantly reinterpreting the classics of a community's culture in order to achieve social change. The classics and the tradition they represent are not criticized; rather, they are used to criticize the society.

Habermas rejects rhetoric to replace it with scientific reason operating on a pyschoanalytical model. Gadamer rejects rhetoric to replace it with philosophical reason operating on a model drawn from Socratic dialogue. The latter sees hermeneutics operating only at an individual level, but at that level it can reevaluate tradition while seeking what is true in tradition. In this respect Gadamer resembles Vico in his reverence for tradition and the classics. Habermas, on the other hand, resembles Vico in his determination to account for social change. Habermas insists on making the interpretation of culture serve social ends, but ends determined not by the culture but by those privy to Marx's understanding of materialism. Vico's notion of *sensus communis* accounts for substantial social change within the culture, that is, the culture retains its own identity and sees itself as making the changes, rather than having them imported by those who possess Habermas's "emancipatory praxis" or some other form of privileged information. Vico is able to incorporate such an account of social change because of the public, oral nature of his idea of *sensus communis*.

SENSUS COMMUNIS, HERMENEUTICS, AND NATURAL LAW

Gadamer attempts to mediate between the Platonic view (tradition as uncritical *doxa*) and the Enlightenment view (tradition as false). Actually, however, his attempt to mediate fails. He truncates *sensus communis* from judgment and thus involves himself in an epistemological cul de sac, and he severs the classic and authority from their rhetorical roots.

Given the terms of this dilemma, Vico's idea of *sensus communis* offers a better mediating position than Gadamer's. On the one hand, it provides a coherent theory of truth derived from the tradition of rhetoric. On the other hand, it provides leverage on social praxis. To this extent, *sensus communis*'s relation to truth seems to participate in the philosophy of pragmatism developed by Peirce and Dewey, as noted by John Michael Krois (1981). This sort of pragmatic approach to truth also brings Vico's *sensus communis* into the orbit of social praxis. Truth is what works, not in some crude utilitarian sense, but in the rhetorical sense, that is, truth is what *makes* sense out of a new problem or situation. Hence the rhetorical tradition, and Vico's *sensus communis* derived from it, is effective in the social and political sphere, seeking to justify change within tradition.

Vico traces the effectiveness of rhetoric in the political and social sphere to natural law, and, although Vico's idea of natural law is less rigid than the received notion, his commitment to natural law separates him from Gadamer and Habermas more decisively than his similarities to their thinking seem to unite him to them.

The title of the first edition of the *New Science* was *Principles of a New Science Concerning the Nature of Nations, by which Are Found the Principles of Another System of the Natural Law of the Gentes*. Although he dropped the reference to a new system of natural law from the title of subsequent editions, Vico still intended the *New Science* to be an exposition of how natural law worked in history. As he states in the "Idea of the Work": "This New Science studies the common nature of nations in the light of divine providence, discovers the origins of institutions, divine and human, among the gentile nations, and thereby establishes a system of the natural law of the gentes, which proceeds with the greatest equality and constancy through the three ages which the Egyptians handed down to us as the three periods through which the world had passed up to their time" (31).

Thus Vico is arguing that the "poetic logic" with which the *sensus communis* adapts itself to various "needs and utilities" in the three stages of culture is actually a process of natural law. The *sensus communis,* as Leon Pompa puts it, "harnesses" natural law and men, combines them in "the beliefs that men develop in their institutional roles" (1975, 38).

Gadamer, as we have seen, is extremely cautious of accepting any theory of language or *sensus communis* that might entail a relation to natural law. He repeats this caution in a letter to Richard Bernstein, which the latter published as an appendix to his *Beyond Objectivism and Relativism:* "There is no independent sphere of law or right in Greek culture, just as there is no conception of freedom at all. Nevertheless, we can learn something here—for example, not to fall prey to a dogmatic misuse of natural law arguments" (1983, 265). Obviously "dogmatic use of natural law arguments" would be antithetical to the sort of dialogue Gadamer envisions as the proper mode of hermeneutic inquiry.

Habermas, of course, would also reject natural law because it would participate in the oppressive ideology. The whole thrust of Habermas's critique, or any Marxist critique, is that what is assumed to be "natural" is in fact part of a structure of economic oppression and domination. Both Habermas and Gadamer, however, would conceive natural law as some set of permanently valid, objective norms that hold for all societies at all times. This is the definition arrived at by modern natural law theorists, but it is exactly what Vico did not mean, and what he saw the *New Science* as opposing.

Vico was differentiating himself from the natural law theory that was predominant in his time and that was formulated chiefly by Hugo Grotius. That theory held that primitive peoples everywhere and at all times had a "natural" grasp of the principle of equity. Although

Vico agreed that some sort of normative belief must prevail in any system of social relationships, he maintained that the natural law was different for different stages of development. The principle of equity, which Grotius and others felt was fundamental to natural law, Vico held was articulated by societies only after long struggle. That struggle followed the course of the poetic logic through the three stages of culture and has been analyzed by Mooney (1985, 235–37).

Mooney notes that, for Vico, the first law is the law of force. The primitive nobles secure the law through auspices that they alone control and interpret, and the law is a secret known only to the nobles. After long struggle, the plebs, or commoners, compel the laws to be written down. There follows a period of what Vico calls "heroic jurisprudence," a superstitious observance of the words of the law. As Mooney puts it, "the secrecy of the law is replaced by an arcane jurisprudence. Thus ensues the contest of tongue against code, orator against jurist" (1985, 236). This process gradually leads to the extension of citizenship to all and to the incorporation of natural equity into a jurisprudence that interprets the written code. Only after this happens can we reflect upon the process and become conscious of natural law as an abstract entity.

What is important about this account of natural law is that each stage has a kind of law that is natural to it, and yet each stage is only a stage, containing within itself the impetus to further development. As Amos Funkenstein writes, "Vico insisted that 'natural law' was based neither on social instincts nor on deliberate reasoning or on necessities (or norms) but on the very immanent, regular 'ideal' *process* through which civilization emerges time and again as man's acquired nature" (1976, 210). In short, Vico makes natural law dynamic rather than static, a mode of bringing human nature into being via civilization, as well as a mode of judging human action.

This conception of natural law avoids the "dogmatic natural law arguments" that Gadamer fears because it allows for *sensus communis* to remain stable while it is being reinterpreted constantly in the light of new social exigencies. This is the very process by which natural law develops. However, the process of development is rhetorical and linguistic. Eloquence and rhetoric fuel Vico's dynamic conception of natural law, just as *sensus communis* is its stabilizing agent.

Vichian hermeneutics take place in the public world of rhetorical humanism. Interpretation is always for use in the dialectic by which natural law works to civilize human society. Gadamer's hermeneutic is permanently vulnerable to Habermas's charges because it tries to incorporate dialectic into the act of reading, whereas Vico incorporates hermeneutics into the dialectic of culture. Habermas claims that social praxis should determine the hermeneutical program. For Vico, hermeneutics is praxis, the practice of public eloquence reinterpreting the *sensus communis*. To this extent, Vico both relates hermeneutics to social practice and stabilizes it.

The oral nature of Vico's *sensus communis* provides the sort of holism that permits it to be an agent of both change and stability. That holism combines the judging faculty and the shared moral consensus under one rubric, a combination that makes sense within the dynamics of extemporaneous oral performance. Replacing *sensus communis* in its oral, rhetorical context allows it to combine the functions Gadamer had to separate in order to bring it into the dynamics of reading, separations that left him open to accusations of relativism and irrelevance.

Gadamer's work does not address the issue of the origin of the *sensus communis* and the epistemological status of its *arche*. Nor is this issue ever addressed by the Greek philosophers whom Gadamer so admires and into whose tradition he works so hard to bring hermeneutics. Those philosophers developed their ideas in opposition to rhetoric, and they spent their lives criticizing the unreflective acceptance of *sensus communis,* which they never conceived of relating to any sort of natural law. Vico draws his inspiration, not from Greek philosophy, but from Roman rhetoric. For Vico, rhetoric is "first philosophy," and he places the philosophers, particularly the Greek philosophers, at the end of the process (239). In the *New Science* he calls them "the old men of the nations" (498), and places irony, the trope which figures so prominently in Plato's thought, at the end of the cultural cycle (408).

Do we not see in Gadamer's work, brilliant though it is, another example of what Eliza Butler called "the tyranny of Greece over

Germany"? Gadamer himself never questions the centrality of the Greek philosophical tradition or its suitability as a model of hermeneutics. He does not consider the role of the rhetorical tradition in Western culture except for its role in forming the Greek philosophical tradition. But if we take Gadamer's own theory seriously, then the Roman tradition of *sensus communis,* which Vico explicated so profoundly, could serve to "move the horizon" that constrains Gadamer's hermeneutics.

6   Vico and Derrida on Language

SENSUS COMMUNIS AND METAPHOR

In *Truth and Method,* Gadamer asserts that "The word is not just a sign. In a sense that is hard to grasp it is also something like an image"*(WM* 1975, 394/ *TM* 1975, 377). Gadamer proceeds to explain just how a word is like an image: "A word is not a sign for which one reaches, nor is it a sign that one makes or gives to another. . . . We seek for the right word, ie, the word that really belongs to the object, so that in it the object comes into language. Even if we hold to the view that this does not imply any simple copying, the word is still part of the object in that it is not simply allotted to the object as a sign" *(VM* 1965, 394/ *TM* 1975, 377).

In these words Gadamer challenged the theory of language proposed by Ferdinand de Saussure in his *General Course in Linguistics,* but when he published *Truth and Method* Gadamer could not have foreseen how de Saussure's structural linguistics would permeate French critical theory.

Walter Ong has attacked the structuralist view of language briefly but trenchantly on the grounds that it imports a visual metaphor into the nature of language, a metaphor biased toward print and typography. Ong argues that language is essentially oral and auditory in nature, and that written language must refer to an auditory experience, not a sign, to be intelligible (1982, 75–77). To call words "signs" or language a "system of signs," makes the typographic quality of written language a metaphor for language itself. To an extent, then, Ong has "deconstructed" the metaphor on which French critical theory rests, but he has not developed this insight systematically.

The metaphors one uses to describe language are precisely the issue in a comparison of Derrida and Vico. Derrida operates with (and on) the visual metaphor, the "sign," on which structuralism depends. If we see Derrida's thinking emerging from a long tradition grounded in the Enlightenment, then we may expect Vico's work, directed against Enlightenment theories of language, to provide an oral, rhetorically based counterpart to contemporary French critical thought. In fact, by comparing Vico's thinking on metaphor and writing with that of Jacques Derrida, one can see, first, how Vico can contribute an alternative theory of metaphor, one based on primary rhetoric and its attendant orality; second, how one can suggest the outlines of an alternative theory of writing.

Derrida's well-known essay "White Mythology" (1974) continues the Franco-Italian debate on metaphor, although Derrida reaches conclusions that would have scandalized Bouhours or Boileau. Derrida begins with the presuppositions of structuralist linguistics and proceeds to examine the function of metaphor in philosophical discourse. His first aim is to prove that philosophy is doomed to employ a language in which thinking will always be impeded by metaphor. His second aim is to discover the implications of the inescapability of metaphor for Western metaphysics, an inescapability he links to the so-called transcendental signifier, that presence which seems to insure language against a collapse into relativism, and he concludes that this signifier is a myth and that thus the whole discipline of metaphysics is founded upon a mythical presence that inhabits the really empty space of metaphor. Let us examine how Derrida proceeds to this conclusion and the assumptions and metaphors that control that process.

Derrida begins "White Mythology" by interrogating the most common metaphor for language itself: coins. The wear and tear that metaphors endure in their history is analogous to the wearing down of the face and date on coins. Derrida points out that the eighteenth century held as a commonplace that "at its origins language could have been purely sensory, and that the *etymon* of a primitive meaning, though hidden, can always be determined" (1974, 8). After long use, the metaphoric origins of any word, the comparison originally at its heart, becomes effaced into a "proper" meaning, but the "use" is also a "usury" in that the word acquires more than metaphorical meaning, a kind of linguistic surplus value (1974, 7). This account of metaphor, from sensory beginnings to abstract use, certainly resembles Vico's, but it is precisely this account which Derrida rejects. "If we read in a concept the hidden history of a metaphor, we are giving a privileged position to *diachrony* at the expense of system, and we are putting our money on that *symbolist* conception of language which we have touched on: the link between signifier and signified had to be and to remain, though buried, one of natural necessity, of analogical participation, and of resemblance" (1974, 12–13).

Just as he dismissed the effort to account for any one metaphor historically, so too Derrida dismisses the attempt to arrive at a theory of metaphor: "metaphor remains in all its essential features a classical element of philosophy, a metaphysical concept. It is therefore involved in the field which it would be the purpose of a general "metaphorology" to subsume" (1974, 18).

Derrida argues that there can be no account of metaphor that is not itself metaphorical, and *that* metaphor would not be included in the general account. Hence, theories of metaphor are doomed to incompleteness. But another issue is more central to Derrida's argument: the relation of metaphor to the concept of the *logos* in Western philosophy. Derrida formulates this issue in terms familiar to Vico's readers. He asks, What *logos* is as metaphor? and answers the question himself by pointing to the duplicity in the word *sense,* which can mean a signified (a nonspatial, atemporal content) and its sensible (open to the senses) signifier. Because of this dualism in the heart of meaning itself, Derrida concludes that philosophy cannot really grapple with metaphor. In fact, he points out that philosophical language is permeated with prephilosophical metaphors that encase the problem philosophy would attempt to solve. In the face of this dilemma, Derrida resolves not to analyze metaphor philosophically, but rather to place the concept of metaphor in a larger field of metaphors (1974, 29).

Derrida spends the last half of the essay analyzing what he calls the master metaphor: the sun. He refers to it as the heliotrope, the metaphor to which all other metaphors turn, just as the flower follows the sun across the sky. This elaborate metaphor for metaphor expresses Derrida's conviction that metaphor in philosophic language always implies a presence that the philosophy itself has not established, but which is taken for granted, a sun that illumines language with an unquestioned light: "this is our problem—the theory of metaphor remains a theory of sense and supposes a certain originating naturalness in this figure. How is this possible" (1974, 32)?

Derrida's answer to his own question is mimesis, and he criticizes it. First, he criticizes it for disguising nature: "It surely belongs to *mimesis* that redoubling in *physis,* that point at which nature, veiled by her own act, has not yet recovered her proper nakedness, the very act of her proper self" (1974, 42). By this he means that metaphor can always be false in the sense that it disguises what may be important, that the differences in the two terms of a metaphor may be more significant than the similarities. Second, the statement implies that nature is capable of pure perception, a "proper nakedness" without being covered in the veil of *mimesis,* the same image Bouhours used to describe metaphor in the eighteenth century. Nature's "proper nakedness" is her "proper self," but it is a propriety and a nakedness that has to be "re-covered." Derrida is alluding to the fact that propriety, the proper meaning, is not a given from which the metaphor deviates, but a meaning that must be recovered from the metaphor even as it discloses the nakedness of nature by "recovering" it, that is, covering it over, in another language. Despite all its subtlety the argument still imports the idea of propriety, that Cartesian standard of rational use of language.

Derrida argues next that metaphor's riskiness, its inherent capacity for missing things, is bound to an absence; a metaphor's terms are seldom explicit, but rather implicit, left for the hearer or reader to find. For Vico, this absence is precisely the source of metaphor's power; for Derrida, it makes metaphor epistemologically suspect. He takes Aristotle's example: *sow* is a word meaning to cast seed, but there is no word for the motion of the sun sending out its rays, so we can transfer the "sowing" of seed to the sun. But, as Derrida points out, we have never *seen* the sun sowing rays; the concept is alien to what the sun is seen to do. Rather, someone makes the transference, and this transference depends upon a power of *mimesis,* which itself cannot be taught but is "natural." Hence he concludes that "The genius for *mimesis* can therefore give rise to a language, to a code of controlled substitutions, to the talent and the techniques of rhetoric, to the imitation of genius to the mastery of the ungraspable" (1974, 46).

This concept sounds very much like Vico, yet Derrida adds a caveat that reveals where his analysis is tending—and from where it comes: "In what conditions do we always have another trick up our sleeve" (1974, 46)? The trick turns out to be the sun metaphor itself. Derrida proceeds to deconstruct the master metaphor of the Enlightenment, light itself.

Derrida argues that the whole vocabulary of truth in the Greek philosophical tradition is derived from metaphors of light and sun, for example, *phainesthai* and *aletheia*. But the sun itself is not always present; it moves away and eventually disappears. This movement, says Derrida, is a paradigm of metaphor itself: "And the sun, in this respect, is above all the sensible signifier of what is sensible, the sensible model of the sensible (the Form, paradigm, or parable of the sensible). For these reasons, the orbit of the sun is the trajectory of metaphor" (1974, 52). In the Aristotelian tradition metaphor is described in terms presumed to be non-metaphoric, terms that have proper meanings. But those proper meanings are also metaphoric, inextricably linked to light and the sun, whose trajectory thus becomes an analogue of the "trajectory of metaphor," its constant turning in upon itself when one attempts to define it.

Derrida next turns to his real objective: the deconstruction of the "light" in the "Enlightenment," the intellectual movement which, above all else, eschewed metaphor in favor of proper meanings. "Everything in talk about metaphor which comes through the sign eidos, with the whole system attached to this word, is articulated on the analogy between *our* looking and sensible looking, between the intelligible and the visible sun. The truth of the being that is present is fixed by passing through a detour of tropes in this system" (1974, 55–56).

Eidos, Derrida reminds us, is the Greek term for image, that is, for something visible. An "idea" is something visually present in the mind for which a proper word is thought to exist, but in formulating this proposition one is already using a visual metaphor for thought. Furthermore, this model of metaphor's relation to thought presumes a certain static presence, the "thing" for which the image "stands" and which the word expresses. Hence the "light" of the "Enlightenment" presumes a presence, an idea and its corresponding "thing," a duality that is really only a metaphor itself.

Derrida proposes two alternative attitudes that one could take to the inescapability of metaphor in philosophical language. The first is to seek a return to direct apprehension of presence, "the manifestation of truth as an unveiled presence, to the regaining of language in its fullness without syntax, to a pure calling by name" (1974, 73). Here he is probably referring to Foucault.[1] The second alternative is to dissolve the borders of metaphorical and proper meaning syntactically, that is, of "deploying" a philosophical notion in such a way that the "borders of what is proper for it are torn from it; consequently the reassuring dichotomy between the metaphorical and the proper is exploded" (1974, 74).

The style of "White Mythology" reflects the conclusions and predilections of its author. Derrida is turning the Enlightenment against itself, showing that in its attitude toward metaphor it subverts the metaphor, light, upon which it erected its own philosophical discourse. His style is metaphorical, but self-consciously so. "White Mythology" is a metaphor for the problem he is uncovering: the light that informs Enlightenment epistemology is a metaphor itself, but its brightness covers up the absence behind it, that is, the myth of a presence, a signified without a signifier. "White Mythology" also connotes, of course, the predominance of this epistemology in white Western culture, and it alludes to its role in Western imperialism. Nonetheless, Derrida is still operating with assumptions about metaphor that he inherited from the eighteenth-century rationalist critics whom Vico opposed. In short, Derrida deconstructs Enlightenment epistemology and its theory of metaphor from the inside, basing his claims on the metaphoric structure of Enlightenment and Aristotelian language about metaphor. Vico, on the other hand, develops a theory of metaphor based on entirely different metaphorical language. His theory of metaphor emerges from oral, not visual, analogues for intellect, even though he uses some of the same Aristotelian texts as Derrida. By comparing Vico's writing about metaphor with Derrida's, we can see, first, the historical lines that still control French post-structuralism, and, second, we will discover if rhetoric, as Vico conceived it, has anything to offer to a discussion of metaphor and philosophic discourse.

There are three major differences in Vico's and Derrida's approach to metaphor. First, and most important, Vico develops his theory on an oral/auditory model, deliberately rejecting the visualism of the Enlightenment. Second, Vico proceeds to develop a theory of metaphor diachronically, a procedure Derrida specifically rejects because, he says, it assumes a natural link between signifier and signified. Finally, Vico's theory of metaphor emerges from, and is addressed to, the *sensus communis* rather than beginning, and ending, as Derrida does, with philosophic discourse. These differences, however, imply a great many more, and in exploring these three we can trace the difference in post-structuralist and Vichian views of metaphor and language.

Vico's account of the origin of metaphor is also his account of the origin of religion, language, and the human race itself. It is his account of the imaginative universal of Jove discussed in chapter 4; Jove is a metaphor, a Baroque metaphor, which connects thunder/voice to sky/body. The metaphor features sound rather than sight and interprets sound as the sign of life. Sound comes from the interior of things; it frequently connotes life or animation, as when we feel "spooked" by the sound of the wind in the trees or the creaking of boards. The giants imagine the sky as a person, and thunder as his voice.

The next salient feature of this account is that metaphor gives birth to language, not in speech, but in interpretation. Vico specifically states that language begins with "divination," the art of interpreting the auspices of the gods, rather than with articulate speech. In short, hermeneutics precedes speech.

The final aspect of this account is perhaps the most important. The giants create a metaphor of Jove, but it is only a metaphor from our perspective. The giants do not see it as a metaphor, or rather do not hear it as one. For them, the transfer of meaning that equates thunder with voice and sky with body is an identity, not a metaphor. Derrida comments that the *mimesis* which creates metaphor "does not occur without *theoretical* awareness of resemblance or likeness, that is, of what will always be taken to be the condition of metaphor" (1974, 37). Vico's point is that the giants are incapable of any "theoretical" awareness; they make a transfer of meaning that constitutes an identity they themselves do not perceive as metaphorical at all. This metaphor is, for Vico, the beginning of the *logos,* the concept Derrida claims is the basis of Western metaphysics.

Derrida seems to be tracing Vico's own line of reasoning when he says metaphor comes from man's natural bent to imitation and from pleasure in words of imitation. As he says, *"logos, mimesis,* and *aletheia* become here one and the same possibility"* (1974, 38), which certainly describes the way Vico impacts language, imagination, and truth in the imaginative universal. In Vico's account of the imaginative universal of Jove, then, is a kind of anatomy of the creation of the *logos* and the concomitant logocentrism of metaphor and its use in Western philosophy. What remains to be seen, however, is how Derrida's critique of metaphor can be reconciled with the orality that both he and Vico ascribe to the *arche* of metaphor.

Derrida says that the *logos* is at home only in the *phoné* (sound, voice), but, unlike Vico, he chooses a visual metaphor for metaphor, or rather he adopts and criticizes the metaphor for metaphor that French philosophy inherited from the Enlightenment: the sun. On the other hand, Vico's primal metaphor is thunder. The giants do not name thunder, they interpret it. Its being in the human world is not metaphorical, it is only perceived as the voice of a sky god; it isn't thunder at all. The metaphor is its "proper" meaning, and even that metaphor implies further meanings: that is to say, what the sky god is communicating, for example, anger or commands. Hence the "fall" into metaphor is, for Vico, quite natural. There are no proper meanings for him either; only his view that language contains the *logos* and in fact starts with it. But for Vico the *logos,* born in imagination and metaphor, is something entirely different from Derrida's conception of it. Vico gives an account of how that "presence" of *logos* came into being in language.

Vico's account of *logos* is that it is a *mythos,* which, as he says, is the same as *fabula* and denotes a "true narration." Every metaphor, Vico says, is a "fable in brief" *(New Science* 404), that is, every metaphor narrates a predication based on similarities, a proposition that makes a claim on our credibility and calls for our assent. But even more, the metaphor, as a fable, implies a story, a narration whose meanings are implied and seemingly infinite in the potential for application. I must emphasize both aspects of Vico's definition: a metaphor is both true and a narration. A metaphor is a true story that has not yet ended.

What kind of predication is involved in a metaphor? For Derrida, metaphor is a trope of resemblance that veils a presence not really there, an ontology that is itself only metaphoric. Vico's definition of metaphor, far from contradicting such a claim, seems to make it explicit. For Vico, the predication at the heart of every metaphor, especially the imaginative universals, is the predication of being. Vico is quite prepared to say that a metaphor predicates being of an individual; more precisely, it predicates of a particular a universal which is not "proper." To say "My love is a red rose" does not mean that she is similar to a rose, or that she looks like or smells like a rose. These are similes. Rather it means that the essence of roseness is predicated of an individual human being. Obviously, many characteristics of roses are not "proper" to humans, for example, humans do not have petals. The metaphor's force, however, does not depend upon propriety or impropriety, but upon the force of the predication of being; rose essence is predicated of a human.

Enlightenment critics like Bouhours, of course, pointed out that in any metaphor that was important, the accidental differences did matter. They were the imposed, "improper" meanings. But Vico's description of the *arche* of language in metaphor precludes this critique because, for the giants, there could be no proper meaning. The imaginative universal of Jove predicated being of God; the sky was god; divinity was the sky's proper meaning; anger was the proper meaning of its thunder. Vico, then, does not "veil" the ontology implicit in metaphor, rather, he unveils it and proceeds to trace how it operates in human language.

Vico's "poetic logic" traces the emergence of language and *sensus communis* from the imaginative universals, the first metaphors. This is exactly what Derrida chose not to do: "our task is not to trace back the function of a concept along a line to the etymology of the word" (1974, 54). Derrida only sees the concept, the proper meaning of an abstract term, as emerging from a metaphoric etymology. However, Vico does not, by our standards, really trace words back to their metaphoric roots, either. The imaginative universal should not be confused with some sort of linguistic root. Vico's own etymologies are frequently ludicrous by modern standards, and Tullio de Mauro has pointed out that Vico's relevance to the discipline of historical linguistics is still disputed (1969). What is significant about Vico's "etymologies" is that he tries to articulate the accumulated connotations of words. While he himself may have thought these connotations to be historical, we can see that they are rhetorical definitions of the sort Quintillian described. The "etymologies" are derived with an argumentative purpose in mind: to confute the belief in conventionalism. Vico does this by tracing how certain words like *lex* acquired their connotations from concrete social circumstances, rather than from arbitrary conventions. His theory of language thus begins with *mythos,* the true narration which cannot be verified.

Vico actually articulates a myth of language rather than a history of it. Histories always have an arbitrary starting point. Any event or sequence of events can be seen to emerge from a "starting point," but that point always has a history too, and so on ad infinitum. To deal with origins, in the absolute sense, always involves one in myth, that is, a beginning that has no history itself. Vico is using metaphor as that mythic origin, and in fact he states that metaphor is a *mythos.* Hence, Vico has taken the origin of language and metaphor out of history and located it in the time before time, that *in illo tempore* in which all myths happen. But once metaphor is there, once the imaginative universal has come into being with the manifestation of the holy, then time begins, and language begins to exist in it. This account of the imaginative universals, their relation to the *sensus communis,* and the interaction of each within the poetic logic was described in chapter 4. Here it is necessary to highlight the salient differences between the poetic logic and the way Derrida describes metaphor operating.

The first thing that must be noted about the poetic logic is that it does not develop completely within language, that is, the poetic logic is not a system of signs that mediates between signifiers and signified. Vico makes it clear that the development of language from imaginative universals proceeds through the mediation of rhetoric and social institutions. Language develops in response to social praxis. The tropes of resemblance that characterize the stages of the poetic logic, metonymy and synecdoche, emerge out of the original metaphoric sense of language, a sense grounded in sensation itself. Those tropes, however, shape and form social institutions to meet certain exigencies that caused eloquence to discover or "invent" them in the first place. This account of the emergence of new meanings involves both physical and social reality and is not restricted to permutations within a sign system.

Vico's way of describing the relation of metaphor to physical reality also differs sharply from Derrida's account. For Vico, the natural world does not exist until it is incorporated into metaphor. After hearing the thunder, Vico says, the giants "raised their eyes and became aware of the sky" which they immediately incorporated in the metaphor of Jove *(New Science* 377). Metaphor follows sight, but sight follows sound. Nature is heard before it is seen, and when it is seen it is immediately visualized as animate; its first being is divine. Derrida, on the other hand, presumes the scientific view of nature as normative and primary. The moment in which nature is incorporated into metaphor is, for Derrida, "that point at which nature, veiled by her own act, has not yet recovered her proper nakedness, the very act of her proper self" (1974, 42). Vico, however, does not place this normative status in the beginning of the metaphoric process, but at the end. For Vico, humanity needs eons of development to see nature as naked, a vision which, for Derrida, is primary and proper.

Vico places the philosophers at the end of the cultural cycle. So, too, their language, the language of abstract ideas, comes at the end of cultural development, the culmination of the gradual weaning away of the mind from images of sense. Nonetheless, the *sensus communis* remains impacted in language and institutions, at hand for eloquent discourse to shape new institutions and new opinions. The cultural cycles develop the *sensus communis* out of the common sensuality implicit in the imaginative universals. Vico envisions the procedure operating diachronically, but it is incorrect to envision it as operating within a system of signs. Nor is it correct to envision it operating in exclusive stages. The way Vico describes the *sensus communis* and its relation to tropes, and eloquence in general, shows how an oral conception of language can qualify Derrida's conclusions about how metaphor operates in philosophic discourse.

Derrida begins Section V of "White Mythology" with a conclusion with which Vico would certainly disagree: "Classical rhetoric, then, is incorporated in that mass within which the text of philosophy is marked off, and can be given no position of control over that mass" (1974, 60). Derrida is primarily thinking of secondary rhetoric, the compilation of tropes and schemes for study. Vico would conceive of rhetoric as preparation for eloquent performance. Second, Derrida is conceiving of the "mass" of language as a sign system over which no art of rhetoric could exercise control because it would be part of that mass. But Vico conceives of the "mass" of language within which rhetoric and philosophy are inscribed, if he would conceive of it at all, as the *sensus communis,* and that is more than just a sign system. It is a bed rock of intelligible, affective meaning incorporated in language and expressed in institutions. *Sensus communis* cannot exist exclusively in language. Because *sensus communis* originates in the principle of *verum-certum,* it is "expressed" as Vico puts it, in the institutions of a nation, that is, the truth of metaphor is made in the life of the community, in its institutions. *Sensus communis* is the way language relates to public life and its institutional and ethical activity, or rather, it enables humans to use language to modify and adapt institutions, a use Vico always envisions as occurring in the public arena.

The eloquence with which the *sensus communis* is marshaled involves, of course, the use of metaphor and other tropes. These tropes, as Vico explains in both the *De nostri* and the *New Science,* refocus the *sensus communis* on new problems, modifying institutions or creating new ones. The *verum-certum* principle keeps the tropes from being merely a figuration within a sign system. Rather, because of that principle, the tropes can actually keep language related to the real world.

Within Vico's concept of metaphor, *sensus communis* is the "presence" that constitutes metaphor as the *logos,* that is, *sensus communis* is constituted by the "true narration," which first gives form to the common sensuality with which a human community perceives the natural world and proceeds to make a place for itself in it. But to call the *sensus communis* a presence is to employ Derrida's visual metaphor. *Sensus communis* exists orally and aurally in language. It does not denote the reification of being as a visible object, but rather connotes the existence of being as an interiority, that which utters (outers) a sound. Vico's thinking about metaphor is not "logocentric" but "logosemous."

Vico continues his "logosemous" thinking when he discusses the actual procedure of the poetic logic. He points out that the language, religion, and writing "proper" to each stage can actually exist during any stage and, in fact, all forms probably do exist in each state *(New Science* 412, 446, 629). When Vico describes the properties of each age, he does not intend them to be exclusive or exhaustive descriptions, as Derrida intends when he discusses the "proper" meaning of the terms of a metaphor. Rather, Vico means that the social relations, religion, language, writing, and law in each stage can be described in terms of its proper trope.

In a sense, then, Vico's theory of metaphor and poetic logic admits of a kind of relativism, but it is radically different from the relativism implied in deconstruction. For Derrida, metaphor is "hollow," its "sides" constantly "reflecting" each other and thus blinding us to the vacancy at its heart. Philosophic terms are relative in that they refer only to other signifiers, which are themselves metaphors from which the illusion of being has been dispelled. For Vico also, metaphor lies at the heart of language, including philosophic discourse. But at the heart of metaphor lies the *sensus communis*. That sense keeps metaphor, and all eloquent speech, relative to the real world. This sense develops pari passu with social and political institutions, with public morals and ethics. Its meaning is not atemporal, but incorporates a consistency that lies in the predication of being which animated, in the literal sense, the perception of nature in the imaginative universals. This being is, however, heard rather than visualized. Vico's primal metaphor is a word, not a light. If it is "hollow," it echoes the presence of being with which Divine Providence led the earliest people to human consciousness, and every metaphor still echoes that first thunder.

SENSUS COMMUNIS AND THE
SCENE/SEEN OF WRITING

The second major area of contact between Vico and Derrida is writing. Although Vico's thought was decisively controlled by primary rhetoric, he developed a theory of writing which, like Derrida's, displaced the primacy of the spoken word. Derrida developed his theory of writing in his *Of Grammatology* (1976) and *Disseminations* (1981), but he made the most trenchant and clear statement of his ideas in an article in *Glyph One* (1977) entitled "Signature Event Context." That article can provide valuable help in understanding the other two larger, and more difficult, works.

The first of these, *Of Grammatology,* is significant because Derrida mentions Vico. For example, Derrida distinguishes Rousseau's theory of the noun from Vico's, saying that for Rousseau the noun cannot stand alone but must develop along with the verb, whereas for Vico, the noun is penultimate, coming at the end of linguistic development, just before verbs (1976, 279). While thus using Vico as a kind of straw man to illustrate Rousseau's theories, Derrida does not refer to some rather striking similarities between Vico and Rousseau's theory of the origin of language.

The most obvious similarity is that Rousseau replicates Vico's three stages of language corresponding to the three stages of society. Derrida's commentary on this part of the *Discourse* does not mention Vico, but rather deconstructs the logocentrism implicit in Rousseau's account. He focuses on the ambiguity of Rousseau's use of the term *barbarian,* which can have a rigorous, technical meaning or simply the general meaning of a dispersed, disorganized culture. According to Rousseau, barbarians in the first sense have writing; those in the latter sense do not. This contradiction causes Derrida considerable consternation, but he rescues Rousseau by relating script to political organization and claiming that all prior stages of writing may exist in any one stage of society (1976, 294).

The upshot of Derrida's deconstruction of the *Discourse* is the *supplément,* that extra dimension of meaning added to the sign system when it becomes capable of phonetic transcription. Derrida links this *supplément* to the presence of being in Western metaphysics as well as to the full development of law and politics. The *supplément* allows a sign to be itself a signified, as when a spoken word is signified by a written one. However, this "play" of *supplément,* as Derrida calls it, always allows for the possibility of regression, or rather of the temptation to regression, to that earlier metaphoric stage when meaning was univocal. Derrida invokes Vico to illustrate the potential danger: "This play of the supplement, the always open possibility of a catastrophic regression and the annulment of progress, recalls not only Vico's *ricorsi.* Conjugated with what we have called geometric regression, it makes history escape an infinite teleology of the Hegelian type" (1976, 298).

The *ricorsi* becomes for Derrida the attempt to bring back to language that "presence" that existed at its origin, the obliteration of any distance between the signifier and the signified, which Derrida says is illustrated by making the spoken word normative and the written word derivative. The spoken word presents its meaning simultaneous with thought and intention. The written word always implies distance between the written sign and the spoken sign, the *supplément,* and it implies the absence of the speaker and his or her intention, the *différence* between the fully present meaning and intention of the speaker and the deferred meaning and intention of writing. Derrida's theory of writing aims to show that even speaking, orality itself, has the characteristics of writing, and that writing, thus conceived, disestablishes the metaphysical underpinnings of Western thought that are constructed out of the presence of being assumed in the oral model of language.

The real issue then becomes how Derrida can establish that orality has the characteristics of writing. He bases his argument on iteration, which he describes as follows: "In order for my 'written communication' to retain its function as writing, i.e., its readability, it must remain readable despite the absolute disappearance of any receiver, determined in general. My communication must be repeatable—iterable—in the absolute absence of the receiver or of any empirically determinable collectivity of receivers. . . . A writing that is not structurally readable—iterable—beyond the death of the addressee would not be writing" (1977, 179–80). Having defined iteration as the essential characteristic of writing, Derrida proceeds to argue that iteration is also essential to spoken language:

Through empirical variations of tone, voice, etc., possibly of a certain accent, for example, we must be able to recognize the identity, roughly speaking, of a signifying form. Why is this identity paradoxically the division of dissociation of itself, which will make of this phonic sign a grapheme? Because this unity of the signifying form only constitutes itself by virtue of its iterability, by the possibility of its being repeated in the absence not only of its "referent," which is self-evident, but in the absence of a determinate signified or of the intention of actual signification as well as of all intention of present communication. This structural possibility of being weaned from the referent or from the signified (hence from communication and from its context) seems to me to make every mark, including those which are oral, a grapheme in general. . . . (1977, 183)

Language itself, to be language, must be conceived as repeatable, that is, words and structures have a large number of potential applications independent of any of their actual referents and contexts. To this extent, then, spoken language is "graphemic"; it participates in the form of writing.

In the *New Science* Vico makes a statement that Derrida echoes throughout his work. He asserts that writing came before speaking.

the difficulty as to the manner of their [letters] origin was created by scholars themselves, all of whom regarded the origin of letters as a separate question from that of the origin of languages, whereas the two were by nature conjoined. And they should have made out as much from the words "grammar" and "characters." From the former, because grammar is defined as the art of speaking, yet *grammata* are letters, so that grammar should have been defined as the art of writing. So, indeed it was defined by Aristotle [*Topics* 142b 31], and so in fact it originally was; for all nations began to speak by writing, since all were originally mute. "Character," on the other hand, means idea, form model, and certainly poetic characters came before those of articulate sounds [that is, before alphabetic characters]. (429).

Vico conflates the origin of writing and the origin of language and determines to treat them as one question. He already implies a denial of the assumption that writing is the transcription of a previously existing speech. Vico rather searches for the origin of both language and letters in the same *arche,* and he posits it in the age of metaphor, the first stage of human culture. His account of "writing" at that stage, however, makes it clear that his notion of it is far different from what we mean by it, or from what Derrida means by it. That difference is highlighted by how Vico and Derrida regarded hieroglyphics.

First, Vico says that man was originally mute and communicated by "gestures or objects that have natural relations to the ideas they wish to signify" (*New Science* 225), for example, a stalk of wheat would represent a year. He argued that all nations spoke with hieroglyphs "in the time of their first barbarism," that is, they "spoke" by actually using gestures or displaying physical objects (226). Derrida likewise, following Condillac and Rousseau, posits a hieroglyphic beginning to writing (1976, 283–84). However, Derrida denies that the first hieroglyphs actually bore relations to what they represented. Rather, he claims that the first hieroglyphs represented things themselves, that is, a picture of a stalk of wheat represented wheat. Of course this precludes people "speaking" in hieroglyphs. First, he analyzes this hieroglyphic writing as already positing the *supplément,* because the thing represented is not actually there, only the picture is. And second, he argues that hieroglyphic writing has "no recourse to convention" (1976, 292). Only ideograms have the potential for conventionality because they paint "sounds but without splitting up words and propositions" (293).

In this account Derrida excludes the hieroglyph because it does not lend itself to the sort of operations which, since de Saussure, have come to define language. Another way of putting it would be to say that, in his account of hieroglyphs and ideograms, Derrida imports visual space into "metaphoricity," that is, he argues that the metaphor which is writing is a conscious one, that the conscious act which creates writing is an act of distinction.

Vico's account of hieroglyphics features the act of combination, following the tradition of Baroque aesthetics. He equates the hieroglyphs with the imaginative universals, the primal categories of the imagination, first developed in response to the sacred and then expanded in the age of heroes. For Vico, the hieroglyph pictorially represents what the mind grasps as truth; the hieroglyph does not represent an object, as it does for Derrida, but a proposition impacted in a metaphor, the visual equivalent of the Baroque conceit. This sort of hieroglyph represents reality, not language, just as thunder really was the voice of God for the giants, not a metaphor for the voice of God. The metaphoric level has no articulate language to represent. Furthermore, writing must include not only drawing or making other marks, but also gestures or the use of physical objects to convey meaning. What Vico means by writing preceding articulate language is that communication at the metaphoric level is constituted by perceived natural similarities between signifier and signified, before the arbitrary relation of signifier and signified that constitutes language had developed.

Vico's claim for the priority of writing is more radical than Derrida's and is based precisely where Derrida says the specious priority of speech lies: in the claim of natural similarity, the mimetic quality of the signifier. Derrida, on the other hand, bases writing's claim in the iterability of the sign which, he says, shows that it is *différence,* not similarity, which characterizes writing. The two positions could not be more opposed on this point, yet their opposition is dialectical. If Derrida can claim that writing necessarily implies *différence,* Vico can claim that even *différence* must imply similarity. The conceptual identity of signifier and signified is grounded in a natural similarity. This similarity reflects precisely the condition of the metaphoric society—a commonwealth, a society based on similarities and equalities, in other words, a golden age in which everything is what it seems to be. There is no displacement of meaning between signifier and signified, or between man and gods.

The displacement occurs, says Vico, when the stronger appropriate to themselves the power of interpreting the sacred. Then these few become heroes, not merely the strongest men, but the only men, or rather they become godlike while the rest of society is composed of "mere mortals." Their physical strength is complemented by the special relation to the divinity. These heroes wrote a peculiar esoteric language which Vico calls "heroic emblems": "heroic emblems which must have been the mute comparisons which Homer calls semata (the signs in which the heroes wrote). In consequence they must have been metaphors, images, similitudes or comparisons which, having passed into articulate speech, supplied all the resources of poetic expression" (*New Science* 438).

This passage is remarkable for two reasons. First, Vico says that written signs passed into articulate speech, thus reversing not only the chronology, but also the procedure in which we have usually conceptualized the relation of writing and speaking, and second, that these written signs "supplied the resources for poetic expression." First we must note that Vico is still using "writing" in the expanded sense of any gesture or object, but the objects and gestures now seem to participate in a more complex communication act. While in the metaphoric stage the signifiers were identified with the signifieds by virtue of a natural similarity—for example, the sky *was* Jove—in the heroic stage there is consciousness of a difference—for example, the heroes are similar to other men but different in that they participate in some quality like *arete*. Such an interpretation is consistent with Vico's description of the second stage of culture, which he describes in terms of metonymy, a recognition of difference.

The "heroic emblems" are the "resources of poetic expression." In another place Vico says the "heroic characters are the imaginative universals themselves" (*New Science* 934). This statement may become clearer, and its relation to the issue of hieroglyphs and writing will be illuminated, if we note the way Vico exploits the various meanings of the word *character*. The imaginative universal is a character in the sense that it is a person, like Achilles, Odysseus, or Jove himself. But "character" also denotes a name. As Vico explains, "Among the Greeks 'name' and 'character' had the same meaning, so that the Church Fathers used indiscriminately the two expressions *de divinis characteribus* and *de divinis nominibus*. 'Name' and 'definition' have also the same meaning; thus in rhetoric, under the head of *quaestio nominis* we find a search for the definition of the fact . . ." *(New Science* 433).

Finally, a character is that which the brave man inscribes or impresses onto his personality. To be brave is to be Achilles. In imitating Achilles, of course, the hero makes a name for himself. To this extent "character" can exist before the linguistic conceptualization of its attributes. This is what Vico means when he describes the *semata* which the heroes wrote before they passed into articulate speech. The writing is prior in terms of this mimetic process, this inscribing or impressing of the character, not in terms of the iterability of a word. These characters (not words) or hieroglyphs are the imaginative universals. The heroes differentiated themselves from the "mere man" by replicating the posture, the attitudes, and the gestures of those characters. In Vico's view, the heroes maintained their difference from "mere men" by acting out these imaginative universals. Hence, at this stage "writing," that is, inscribing in action and making a name, was an "other creating" activity. It maintained and circumscribed the essential differentiation of the heroes and the plebs.

The difference between heroes and plebs, maintained by the imaginative universals, gives way to an identity based on an abstract genus of which both classes are species. This movement toward commonality is always a taking of power by the plebs in virtue of a new classification, which they initiate through articulate, eloquent discourse. As we saw in chapter 4, Vico's own example of such a social change was the moment when the Roman plebs gained access to the auspices and thus were allowed to legitimize their marriages, giving them rights of inheritance and participation in the life of the republic. The salient point is that Vico introduces alphabetic literacy and articulate speech as proper to the age of men. Nor is it adventitious, as we shall see, that this transformation is accomplished by eloquence.

In describing the movement from heroic to synecdochic age, Vico continues to treat the origin of writing and the origin of language as a single question.

> Finally there were invented the vulgar characters which went with the vulgar language. The latter are composed of words which are genera, as it were, of the particulars previously employed in the heroic languages; as to repeat an example cited above [460], out of the heroic phrase "The blood boils in my heart" they made the word "I am angry." In like fashion, of a hundred and twenty thousand hieroglyphic characters (the number still used, for example, by the Chinese), they made a few letters, to which, as to genera, they reduced the hundred and twenty thousand words (of which the Chinese language is composed). *(New Science* 935)

While we may smile at Vico's naive examples in this passage, there is some truth in the idea that the development of alphabetic literacy is analogous to and consonant with the development of abstract thought (Havelock 1963; Ong 1982). But such literacy is not accompanied, in Vico's view, by any sort of elitist power, as Derrida claims (1976, 301–2). On the contrary, Vico calls alphabetic literacy "vulgar." In another passage he says that "hieroglyphs and heroic letters were reduced to a few vulgar letters, as genera assimilating innumerable diverse articulate sounds, a feat requiring consummate genius. By means of these vulgar genera, both of words and letters, the minds of peoples grew quicker and developed powers of abstraction, and the way was thus prepared for the coming of the philosophers, who formed intelligible genera" *(New Science* 460).

For Vico, the development of alphabetic literacy is a leveling process that helps overcome the rigid distinctions of the heroic society. He says that vulgar speech and letters are the rights of the people, and in another passage he maintains that "Such language and letters [vulgar] were under the sovereignty of the vulgar of the various peoples, whence both are called vulgar. In virtue of this sovereignty over language and letters the free people must also be masters of their laws, for they impose on the laws the senses in which they constrain the powerful to observe them, even against their will . . ." *(New Science* 936). Vico says here that the language of the people controls the meaning of the laws, and he implies that those laws are interpreted in the light of the common language rather than in the privileged or arcane language of the heroes.

The age of men corresponds to the common notion of civilization. It is articulate, literate, and thus corresponds to the sort of context in which Derrida begins his analysis of language and writing. For Derrida, literacy is a civilizing agent. But Vico spends little time describing how writing works in the age of men. Rather, he describes this age as operating rhetorically. For example, note how the heroic age and the age of men deal with law cases. In the heroic age, Vico describes how Roman law plaintiffs were required to state their cases in precise formulas to make their cases fit the law. In the age of men, however, the laws were bent to achieve equity. This bending (for Vico jurisprudence) is accomplished through Roman legal oratory *(New Science* 939–41). In short, the most important thing about the age of men is not the emergence of alphabetic literacy, but the emergence of rhetoric as the art of persuasion. I believe that this is the most fundamental difference between Vico's ideal of civilization and Derrida's—and our own; for Vico, civilization is not literate but rhetorical.

What is important is that Vico reverses the usual idea of the relation of writing and rhetoric. The Enlightenment thinkers, like Locke and Descartes, agreed on little more emphatically than their hatred of rhetoric and their substitution of clarity and order for rhetorical style. This duality was enshrined as the attribute of written prose and defined against the tradition of humanist rhetoric. But for Vico, writing created rhetoric as an art of persuasion. For Vico, therefore, the "language of men" controls the sense of the written word and the written word becomes that on which new meaning is inscribed, and that constantly created new meaning is, in fact, created by the rhetorically trained mind operating in the public arena.

Vico saw rhetoric as the way a literate society disciplines itself to direct its linguistic traditions to the solutions of the new challenges inherent in social complexity. Eloquence can only emerge from a mind disciplined in the art of rhetoric, steeped in images, symbols, structures, and values of the linguistic heritage and trained to apply them.

Vico anticipates modern structuralist and post-structuralist thought by defining writing in terms of inscription and holds for a kind of writing proper to every sociocultural stage. Alphabetic literacy is indeed one of these stages, but the mode by which this stage maintains itself and furthers itself is rhetoric, not merely literacy. Rhetoric, as Vico uses the term, requires literacy, but requires it precisely by way of gaining access to the preliterate *arche* of language, the oral, performative level, which Vico maintains perdures from the primitive and gives language its power to persuade.

Thus Vico presents a complex system of cultural hermeneutics based on the simultaneous emergence (and parallel development) of language and literacy. He anticipates Derrida's insights, but does so from within the rhetorical tradition rather than by turning the Enlightenment tradition against itself. Vico criticizes any theory of language that argues for the primacy of orality, but the critique is based in metaphoricity and similarity, rather than, like Derrida's, in *supplément* and *différence*.

This difference, however, is crucial, because Vico's thinking emerges from the tradition of Italian civic humanism and is wedded to the world of practical politics. His rhetoric is the rhetoric of public language doing things in the public world. Derrida, deconstructing the hypervisualism of Enlightenment thinking, stays nonetheless in the isolate world of philosophical discourse. He writes critiques that disestablish but do not build. From Derrida's perspective, Vico is still operating from the logocentrism that maintains and uses power. Vico, I am sure, would not deny this, but would only point to the potential debilitating effects of deconstruction on decision making, and he would consign Derrida to that "barbarism of reflection," which he says characterizes the corruption of the *sensus communis*.

Derrida addresses the same issues as Vico's Enlightenment opponents: the nature of metaphor and the impact of writing upon our concept of reason. He founds his critique of those Enlightenment positions on the inherent contradictions within that tradition. What Vico's concept of *sensus communis* contributes to this critique is, first, to remind us that Derrida is in fact operating within a long critical discussion; second, that humanist rhetoric may offer an alternative ground for a critique of Enlightenment philosophy; and finally, that the object of Derrida's attack, logocentrism or the "metaphysics of presence," has its roots in the rhetorical tradition and may be defensible within that tradition.

First, and most important, the poetic logic allows for a critique of the interaction of power and language. Vico's *New Science* attempted such a critique, but with the tools available to eighteenth-century analysis. Vico's attempt to describe various social phenomena in terms of the rhetorical tropes was doomed because of his inadequate information about other cultures. But using the tropes as a schema for analyzing constellations of power may be fruitful. Vico's poetic logic offers the possibility of articulating such critiques from within the humanist tradition rather than from outside it as Derrida or Marxist critics like Habermas have done. They use the human sciences, especially psychoanalysis, for their methodologies. Vico's poetic logic offers an alternative method founded on the rhetorical tradition.

While Vico's idea of *sensus communis* offers possibilities for a critique of language and power, it also offers powerful arguments for affirming the essential relationship between language and metaphysics. *Sensus communis* not only makes the poetic logic possible, and thus also makes possible a social critique, but it also explains how the "metaphysic of presence" came to inhabit language so that language is essentially related to social structure. In short, what makes the critique possible also ensures its positive relevance. Or, to put it another way, the *sensus communis* must embrace even the critique if that critique is to be intelligible, much less relevant or successful.

7 Conclusion: Ethics, Rhetoric,
and Sensus Communis

Gadamer has been accused of relativism, and Derrida has consciously espoused it, but Vico's concept of *sensus communis* challenges our received notions of relativism. It says that community must have some shared values, some limits to its tolerance of differences, and it requires that this limit exist not merely in theory but in practice: in education, in law, and in politics. *Sensus communis* is grounded in the language, literature, and institutions of a community and relates to the community's political and social world, a relation that is consensual and concrete. *Sensus communis* provides a historical continuity within which the community can interpret its own policies and make its own decisions. Because of these characteristics, *sensus communis* is not amenable to ethical relativism.

Gadamer and Derrida each pursue a particular philosophical tradition to its logical conclusions: Gadamer the Socratic-Platonic tradition and Derrida the French Enlightenment tradition. Both attempt to investigate their tradition and to apply it to contemporary concerns in the study of philosophical texts. Both refer to Vico, but Vico himself represents a third tradition: classical and humanist rhetoric. That tradition, and its key concept, *sensus communis,* offers possibilities for a new approach to the problems that Gadamer, Derrida, and others have formulated. Such a new approach, of course, will have its own agenda and its own problems, but it may be more fruitful both intellectually and socially than either post-structuralism or the *Hermeneutikstreit.*

As we have seen in chapters 3 and 4, the key to Vico's concept of *sensus communis* is that he conceived eloquence in terms of extemporaneous oral performance and rhetoric as preparation for such performance. He develops *sensus communis* as an epistemological principle which united imagination, language, and social institutions in a dynamic, holistic relationship analogous to the simultaneity of invention, figurality, and organization that occurs in extemporaneous oral performance. *Sensus communis* becomes for Vico the affective, pre-reflective and somatic quality of language, created when both language and human institutions were formed. It is what makes eloquence possible. With *sensus communis* as an epistemological base, Vico explores the critical and hermeneutic possibilities latent in the rhetorical tradition. These possibilities seem to offer a rich alternative to both the hermeneutics of Gadamer and the post-structuralism of Derrida.

Gadamer's hermeneutics (see chapter 5) attempts to bring Vico's concept of *sensus communis* into the tradition of Greek philosophy, and to make dialectics as practiced by Socrates and Plato the paradigm for reading. Gadamer sees the mission of such a hermeneutic to be the individual's interrogation of the *sensus communis* so that the reader may change his or her own values and prejudices. Such a view both privatizes the *sensus communis* and brings it into full consciousness, two things Vico never did. On the contrary, Vico grounded the *sensus communis* in the somatic nature of language that an individual interiorizes, but which is always greater than self and not totally accessible to any conscious act. For Vico, *sensus communis* is what dialogue happens *in* as well as what it can be about.

Gadamer's privatization of *sensus communis* led Habermas to criticize Gadamer's hermeneutic as socially irrelevant, but Vico's original concept of *sensus communis* provides more critical leverage on social reality than Gadamer's revised version of it. Vico's poetic logic uses the rhetorical tropes to describe how the *sensus communis* allows for social innovation and adaptation and the creation of new institutions, while at the same time guaranteeing social continuity. Thus Vico's *sensus communis* offers a kind of hermeneutic *tertium quid* between Gadamer's private hermeneutics and Habermas's radical, social hermeneutics.

While Gadamer tried to criticize Enlightenment philosophy from within the Platonic tradition, Derrida's critique of Enlightenment philosophy deconstructs the hypervisualism that informs it. Unlike Gadamer, Derrida works from within the Enlightenment tradition to dismantle its epistemology. He deconstructs the Enlightenment position on metaphor, showing that philosophy cannot escape from metaphor into a discourse of purely "proper" meanings. Furthermore,

Derrida claims that the Enlightenment's central metaphor, light itself, reveals that the predication of being which lies at the heart of metaphor and language itself is really an illusion. Vico, on the other hand, uses the orality inherent in rhetoric to give an account of the origin of language in metaphor and indicate how the relation of the *logos* to being is critical to the origin of human society.

Vico and Derrida take opposing positions on the origin and nature of language, yet these positions lead them to somewhat similar conclusions about the nature of writing. Both agree that there is a sense in which writing preceded spoken language and that contemporary scholars and philosophers (both Vico's and Derrida's contemporaries) tend to oversimplify the simple, chronological sequence in which writing is presumed to follow upon speaking. Yet they arrive at these similar conclusions from opposite starting points. Derrida argues that the nature of the sign itself is repeatability and that thus even spoken signs, to be signs, participate in the nature of writing. Vico, on the other hand, argues that language started with gestures and physical objects that stood for things to which they had some natural similarity. Hence his argument for the primacy of "writing" is natural similarity and mimesis, which Derrida, following de Saussure's theory of arbitrary signification, denies.

Vico's thinking reveals how a rhetorically grounded theory of language can yield critical insights into the nature of writing. Vico's poetic logic provides a schema for tracing how language interacts with social institutions, and Vico shows how every stage of culture has its own proper writing. This view challenges the received idea that literacy is a criterion of civilization. This is one example of how Vico can provide some critical leverage on received notions of literacy, cultural development, and the presumption of Western cultural hegemony.

Vico's influence has been felt by many contemporary thinkers, and their work already anticipates the direction that a Vichian approach to hermeneutics and language would take. However, that influence has been shaped by the division of intellectual disciplines that Vico violently opposed. As a result, Vico's thinking has been partitioned between philosophy and rhetorical theory. The philosophers have raised serious questions about the ethical relevance of the mainstream of modern Western philosophy, while the rhetorical theorists have addressed the issue of whether the rhetorical tradition has anything to contribute to education in the humanities.

The philosophers who are raising issues congenial to Vico's thinking include Richard J. Bernstein, whose critique of Gadamer has been mentioned in chapter 5, Richard Rorty, Bernard Williams, and Alasdair MacIntyre. These four share a conviction that modern philosophy because of its rationalistic definition of reason is helpless in the face of the increasing disintegration of any ethical consensus around which to order an ethical society. They also share some characteristics of Vico's thinking and all appeal to some version of *sensus communis,* although they may not call it that.

In *Philosophy and the Mirror of Nature* (1979) Rorty attacks self-reflectivity in the Western philosophical tradition since Descartes. He castigates modern philosophy's preoccupation with method and epistemology and argues for what he calls "wholehearted behaviorism, naturalism and physicalism" (1979, 373). Rorty denies the mind-body dualism, rejects the whole tradition of philosophy of knowledge which attempted to justify some sort of method for ascertaining objective truth. He argues for what he calls a philosophy of "edification," that is, philosophy conceived as an on-going dialogue that aims to challenge the convictions of its participants and to build new communities that reflect newly made social bonds, bonds which emerge from practice.

Bernstein in *Beyond Objectivism and Relativism* (1983) addresses the relation of science, hermeneutics and praxis by comparing and contrasting the works of Gadamer, Rorty, Habermas, and Hannah Arendt. Bernstein sets up a dialogue among these philosophers and tries to clarify their positions and find common ground. He claims that each of the philosophers presupposes "shared understandings and experience, intersubjective practices, sense of affinity, solidarity, and those tacit affective ties that bind individuals together in a community" (1983, 226). Bernstein here is obviously positing a kind of *sensus communis,* but his account of it makes no mention of language. Nor does he see rhetoric as the tradition that deals with language's relation to politics.

The problem of how philosophy can interact with the community, rather than merely inhabiting the dialogues of philosophers, has been addressed by Bernard Williams in *Ethics and the Limits of Philosophy* (1985), which borrows substantially from Gadamer. But what Williams borrows is exactly what Gadamer has tried to adapt from Vico: "prejudice."

Williams argues that philosophical reflection, including Socratic dialogue, cannot deal effectively with ethical problems. Western philosophy, Williams argues, has ignored the role of intuition in ethical choice. He describes the role intuition plays in ethical choice and argues that intuition is grounded in prejudices: an innate ethical disposition that every individual inherits with his or her culture (1985, 93–119). One suspects that Williams's concept of prejudice is analogous to Vico's *sensus communis,* and the suspicion is confirmed when Williams gives some hypothetical examples of "prejudice." He describes what he calls a "hypertraditional" society, a society in which ethical values are accepted totally without reflection. His description of this ethically naive society is remarkably similar to Vico's description of the age of the heroes (1985, 148f).

Williams continues by claiming that the "prejudices" of a given community pass through stages of consciousness. This claim bears strong resemblance to Vico's *sensus communis* by arguing for stages of ethical and cultural development. But Williams and Vico differ markedly on the origin and nature of the prejudices that form the substrata of community ethics and ethical development. Vico, as we saw in chapter 4, places the origin of the *sensus communis* in the holy and in religion conceived in its root sense of a binding between man and God. Williams dismisses religion as a factor in cultural origins or development and does not discuss the way in which ethical consciousness develops (1985, 96). Vico, on the other hand, envisioned the development of the *sensus communis* through public, eloquent discourse.

As a philosopher, Williams does not address where prejudices come from or how they develop. He is primarily interested, first, in demonstrating their existence, and second, in showing that they work. Williams could claim that the question of origin and the question of social praxis are sociological, not philosophical, questions. But this disciplinary limitation is exactly what Vico opposed, and what his concept of *sensus communis* was supposed to undercut. Williams's work, brilliant though it is, demonstrates clearly the limitations modern philosophy imposes on itself and which Vico worked to transcend.

The most Vichian of current ethicists is certainly Alasdair MacIntyre. His *After Virtue* (1981) and *Whose Justice? Which Rationality?* (1988) attempt to burst the bonds of his own discipline by pointing out the irreducible differences in competing philosophical traditions. Thus he has formulated, without calling it such, an idea of a *sensus communis,* a bedrock of meaning that members of a community share, and which develops or wanes *pari passu* with concrete social praxis.

MacIntyre first articulated this theory in *After Virtue,* where he argues that the ethics of Enlightenment philosophers have failed and have been replaced in the modern world by what he calls "emotivism," that is, the conviction that ethical choice was ultimately traceable to nondiscursive individual preferences (1981, 11–12). Emotivism arose, he argues, because Western philosophy has abandoned the virtues the culture had enshrined in the literary traditions inherited from its heroic age (125–27). It is difficult to imagine a more Vichian *fons et origo* for ethical conduct or reflection. MacIntyre argues that the systematic development of an ethic based on these virtues exists in the Aristotelian tradition. The rejection of that tradition and its concept of the virtues in favor of a Cartesian notion of "virtue" as "right thinking" marked the beginning of the decline of consistent ethical philosophy, a decline that has resulted in our current moral solipsism. MacIntyre does not refer to our condition as "the barbarism of reflection," but he might as well have.

As Kathy Coers has pointed out in her article "Vico and MacIntyre," MacIntyre's thesis in *After Virtue* is "that moral judgments are linguistic survivors from the practices of classical theism that have lost their context" (1986, 133). When the Enlightenment jettisoned that theism, "it forfeited the unified poetic foundation that Aristotle had inherited from the heroic age" (133). In his more recent *Whose Justice? Which Rationality?,* MacIntyre investigates and contrasts the Aristotelian-Thomist position on justice and law with the theory of justice developed during the Scottish Enlightenment. He concludes that ethics, along with a philosophy of justice and of law, emerge only in the interplay of theory and practical reason within the context of specific social problems. He also concludes that the tradition that has been the most successful in meeting the test of practical rationality is the Aristotelian-Thomist synthesis.

MacIntyre argues that practical reason can only operate from within a tradition because only tradition can make social practice intelligible in ethical terms to begin with. He argues further that ethical choice in fact requires some sort of larger political and cultural framework. He goes so far as to argue for the impossibility of completely and accurately translating the tradition of one culture into another (1988, 370–88). A culture's tradition, derived from its heroic age, forms the boundaries of ethical consciousness in the polis. In short, MacIntyre posits something very close to Vico's *sensus communis* as the grounds of the intelligibility of ethical choice in the polis.

Despite these similarities to Vico (who gets two references in each book), MacIntyre completely ignores the rhetorical component of Vico's thought and, indeed, of the traditions he inspects. His treatment of Aristotle draws upon the *Politics* and the *Nichomachean Ethics* and ignores the *Rhetoric*. MacIntyre investigates the Sophists primarily for their influence upon Plato (1988, 47–54), and his summary of the Augustinian tradition ignores Augustine's immersion in the tradition of classical rhetoric (146–63). He compares and contrasts *philosophical* traditions; he does not attend to the rhetorical tradition that formed the context of that practical reason to which he gives so much importance.

Rorty, Williams, Bernstein, and MacIntyre argue for some sort of *sensus communis* that can ground philosophical discussion and keep it related to the real world. Yet none of them refers to the rhetorical tradition. Rhetoric, a discipline informed by historical consensus that limits and informs ethical and political choice, is simply alien to their discussions.

SENSUS COMMUNIS AND RHETORIC THEORY

Modern scholars of rhetoric are as bound by their discipline as modern ethicists are by theirs. For, while they may be able to specify the linguistic component of tradition or prejudice or *sensus communis* and even describe its operation, they are locked out of the conversation on ethics, which continues among philosophers. The division between eloquence and ethics that Vico resisted at the University of Naples continues to have an impact on rhetoricians as well as philosophers.

Most rhetorical theorists remain within the tradition of secondary rhetoric, content to catalogue and schematize the forms of discourse, its arguments and its figures of speech. For example, Walter H. Beale's *A Pragmatic Theory of Rhetoric* (1987) taxonomizes the various genres and appeals that can constitute a discourse, and he develops an innovative schema for the motives of discourse. In presenting his taxonomies Beale is aware of the persistence of oral forms and oral casts of mind within the rhetorical tradition, and he is careful to distinguish not only oral and written forms, but also oral and written formats of the same form. Beale calls his theory "pragmatic," by which he means a taxonomy based on discourse as it is actually spoken or written rather than based on received genres. Beale's focus on performance is his strongest link to the classical-humanist rhetorical tradition, but his analysis draws its philosophical justification from American pragmatism, particularly Dewey and Peirce (1987, 71).

One rhetorical theorist has challenged the hegemony of secondary rhetoric. Richard Lanham, the director of the writing program at UCLA, has formulated a philosophy of rhetoric that is remarkably similar to that of Vico's *Institutiones* and *De nostri*. First, Lanham understands the reemergence of orality as a condition of the postmodern world. He agrees with Walter Ong that electronic media have replaced print as the primary means of communication in most of the world and that a "secondary orality," a cast of mind similar to that of nonliterate peoples, is appearing within literate civilization (Ong 1971, 284–303). Hence Lanham has developed an approach to rhetoric that features those aspects of orality that obtained in the classical tradition.

Second, Lanham makes style and play the foundation of both his theory and his practice. He fosters the development of a nonpurposive, "playful" attitude toward language. Such an attitude, he feels, assists students to interrogate subjects and problems with imagination and flexibility. Lanham wants students to approach rhetoric and writing with the same attitude as they approach their own popular culture. In this respect, Lanham is replicating the approach which directed the activities of the old Roman *grammaticus,* the *magister ludi,* the "master of the game" who conducted the contests and performances of Roman rhetoric students. Such an attitude gave Roman students access to a kind of psychology which they learned in the "speech in character," and Lanham too emphasizes the psychological insights gained from a playful attitude toward language (1983, 42–43 and passim). Lanham also focuses on flexibility in style and audience awareness, both characteristics of orally controlled rhetoric (35–37; 58–71).

Third, Lanham argues that the oscillation between style and seriousness, play and purposefulness, should become the organizing principle of the core curriculum. In short, he argues for making the tension between orally controlled and visually controlled culture the subject of the English curriculum and the humanities' curriculum generally (146). In arguing this approach to the teaching of writing, Lanham concludes that rhetoric must move back to the center of the humanities' curriculum, a thoroughly Vichian position (142).

Lanham calls for a "post-Darwinian humanism," an attitude toward the humanities and human value in general that takes account of the rapidly changing status of human consciousness and the "global village" in which we live (122–43). "Humanism," he says, "amounts to cultural politics" (137). Lanham recommits humanism to public life, a view that certainly seems to put him in Vico's tradition, but he chooses Castiglione's courtier as his model of the humanistically educated man; the choice reveals the difference between Lanham's and Vico's positions.

The courtier is a creature of style; his distinguishing feature is *sprezzatura,* a kind of careless grace, an effortless effort, exhibited even when performing difficult or dangerous tasks. The courtier's eloquence is an eloquence of pleasing. He has the ability to "fit in," as we would say today. He is able to suit himself to any audience or any environment. Such eloquence differs from Vico's idea, however, which features perspicuity and learning, the "heroic mind." To describe the difference another way, Lanham keeps the playfulness of rhetoric but not the purposiveness of eloquence. Vico saw rhetoric as playful training for serious work, work that focused the *sensus communis* on new issues, and the orator can focus the *sensus communis* because he incorporates both the community's literary tradition and its ethical consensus. Castiglione's courtier has, however, no ethical commitment except to please his prince. His education and formation as described by Castiglione, and presumably endorsed by Lanham, exclude any commitment to normative ethical value. Rather, the courtier's flexibility extends to counseling his prince about means and ends without regard to any value higher than honor or success.

Not only does Lanham endorse Castiglione's "flexible" courtier, but he also protests against ethics, by which he means the ethics of formal philosophy, as being too removed from real life to be of any use. For Lanham, ethics presupposes purpose, that is, ethics presupposes that human action must be directed by some sense of purpose outside itself, and it is this sense of purpose that Lanham's rhetorical theory undercuts. Flexible rhetoric requires uncommitted orators.

Unlike Vico, for whom literature was part of the deposit of the *sensus communis,* Lanham argues that literature shows that ethics is too simple to be of any practical value (83–84). Lanham simply ducks the whole issue of rhetoric's relation to ethics by maintaining that "we are good, finally, partly by intuition" (103). He never says what other parts contribute to our being good, or if rhetoric has anything to do with them. In short, Lanham also opts for ethical relativism.

Lanham's "post-Darwinian humanism" seeks a justification for rhetoric in a scientific world view, in this case an evolutionary world view. Lanham is still pursuing the nineteenth- and twentieth-century search for a scientific basis for education, albeit a rhetorical education. Vico, on the other hand, presents *sensus communis* as the basis for a "new science," one founded within the rhetorical tradition. Vico tells us not to seek humanism's justification in science, but that humanism carries its own epistemology and method within the rhetorical tradition.

There is a still sharper contrast between Vico's *sensus communis* and Lanham's humanism, a contrast between evolution and development. Lanham's appeal to "post-Darwinism" indicates a refusal to endorse any values as permanent. Rather, Lanham sees the future as an arena of competing values and ideas, an arena in which the orator must be willing to "play" his part while social forms and commitments evolve without any commitment or assistance on his part. Vico, on the other hand, posits a mythico-religious *arche* for that *sensus communis* which underwrites the community's cultural continuity. The orator actively participates in the *sensus communis* with his eloquence, that is, he assists it to develop. And, according to Vico, it does develop; it does not merely evolve. It changes according to the influence of reasoned eloquence rather than according to unconscious social laws.

What we see today, then, is that Vico's idea of *sensus communis* has been divided along disciplinary lines. Ethics and philosophy have subsumed the aspect of judgment, while rhetoric theory has adopted *sensus communis* as the "standard of eloquence." In the *De nostri,* Vico argues that these two aspects were in fact one thing, viewed either as a faculty or as a standard, which operated simultaneously in oral performance and were developed simultaneously in rhetorical training. Vico opposed the division of rhetoric into discrete disciplines like ethics and law, and the current inability of philosophers like MacIntyre and rhetoricians like Lanham to find common ground justifies his worst fears.

What *sensus communis* provides, and what current ethicists want, is an epistemological principle that relates ethics and hermeneutics to the world of concrete social practice. To get beyond objectivism and relativism, in Bernstein's phrase, means constituting discourse within a consensus, that "spaciousness" to which Weaver referred. But that sort of space, although broad and wide, is limited. What I have tried to show is that, although Vico's idea of *sensus communis* creates the rhetorical "spaciousness" that makes eloquence possible, it also sets a theoretical limit to the potential range of meanings and praxis.

The major philosophical traditions that Gadamer and Derrida represent are traditions formed by literacy and to some extent formed against rhetoric. These traditions incorporated the division between *doxa* and truth, *bon sens* and rhetoric, which have become institutionalized in academic disciplines and impede any attempts at synthesis. By pointing to the holistic nature of *sensus communis,* Vico redraws the boundaries of both community and sense, gives them a different history by giving them a common *arche.*

Vico's concept of *sensus communis* constitutes the sort of epistemological *cum* ethical sense that challenges modern relativism and for which modern ethicists call. It exists, however, not within the tradition of ethics but within the tradition of rhetoric. Our world is shaped by centuries of literacy and its attendant visual analogue for intellect. Contemporary scholars are preoccupied with resolving precisely the split between ethics and public life, education and values, that Vico opposed in the first place. Vico reminds us that our civilization is built upon a *sensus communis* that is essentially oral, communal, and practical, and he challenges us to redraw the cultural history of the West from within its rhetorical tradition rather than from within the traditions of Greek philosophy or Enlightenment rationalism.

Notes

1 ORALITY AND WRITING IN THE HISTORY OF RHETORIC

1. References to the *New Science* are to the English translation *The New Science of Giambattista Vico*, trans. Thomas Bergin and Max Fisch (Ithaca, N.Y.: Cornell University Press, 1944) and are to the paragraph numbers.

2. This does not mean that writing had no effect on the Sophists. Protagoras is credited with contributions to the study of grammar (Beck 1964, 171). Yet his concern for grammar was animated by his desire that his students speak correctly.

3. When discussing Roman rhetoric it is good to remember that the classical texts that come to our minds—Cicero's *Orator, De oratore,* the *Rhetorica ad Herennium,* and Quintillian's *Institutiones oratoriae*—represent ideal descriptions of rhetorical education that were seldom realized. Cicero's portrait of the *doctus orator* in the *Orator* represents his notion of the perfect orator who could marshal every kind of knowledge into arguments for persuading the public to perform good actions. Quintillian's program attempted to realize this ideal, but in fact the schools of the *grammatici* and the rhetors never achieved anything like this ideal and most probably never even attempted to do so. It was the Renaissance humanists who tried to put Cicero and Quintillian into practice.

4. At this point it may be opportune to note something about Roman rhetoric that Bonner comments upon here and there: its connections to the theater. We have already seen that questions of grammar were frequently resolved by referring to the usage of the dramatists whose work existed in more or less permanent texts. More important, however, was the role of dramatics in even the most elementary school exercises. The "speech in character" was a dramatic performance, and poetry was recited "dramatically." Some teachers even invited professional actors to teach their classes and give instruction in proper diction, voice modulation, and even to help students overcome speech impediments (Bonner 1977, 224–26). Even reading aloud was dramatic; the text was interpreted vocally. Bonner cites a letter of Pliny's in which he praises the slave who read to him daily by saying he could easily have been a "comoedius," that is, an actor (1977, 224). What we call today "oral

interpretation" was incorporated at every level of grammatical and rhetorical training. This "theatricality" of rhetoric training was unquestioned in the Roman world and testifies to the essentially oral conception of rhetoric that the Romans had. Later, in the Renaissance, this connection to theater will be recovered, but with rather different results as we shall see.

5. By the time of the Empire, most opportunities for deliberative address had disappeared and courtroom pleading eventually gave way to the submitting of written depositions. The decline of eloquence as a serious force in Roman public life was accompanied by a corresponding increase in its aesthetic status. Going to declamations became widely popular. Public declamations drew large audiences, as did oratorical contests. Rhetorical display was appreciated for its own sake just when Senate speeches and other civil oratory had become a mere "show" behind which stood the real power of the emperor.

6. For a discussion of Augustine's orality see Roy D. DeFerrari, "St. Augustine's Method of Composing and Delivering Sermons," *American Journal of Philology* 43 (1922): 97–123; 193–211.

7. One of the first medieval *ars dictaminis*, the *Dictaminum radii* of Alberic of Monte Cassino in 1087, seems to have been the first treatise to refer to the reader as a *scriptor* rather than as an *orator* [speaker], and it referred to a letter's reader [*lector*] rather than to its hearer [*auditor*] (Murphy 1974, 204). Nonetheless, Alberic's treatise remains close to Roman rhetorical theory. His "art" of letter writing is really Ciceronian rhetoric adapted to epistolary form.

2   ORAL ARENAS IN VICO'S NAPLES

1. The dedication of Florentine humanists to Latin eloquence, and the impact of that dedication on Florentine society, has been studied by Gene Brucker, *The Civic World of Early Renaissance Florence* (Princeton, N.J.: Princeton University Press, 1977). On the other hand, civic humanism never took hold in Venice. Its oligarchical politics stifled any genuine political discourse and restricted eloquence to ceremonial performances. See William J. Bouwsma, *Venice and the Defense of Republican Liberty: Renaissance Values in the Age of the Counter-Reformation* (Berkeley: University of California Press, 1968), and Edward Muir, *Civic Ritual in Renaissance Venice* (Princeton, N.J.: Princeton University Press, 1981).

2. For many decades the classical treatment of Neapolitan history in English was the translation of Benedetto Croce's *Storia del regno di Napoli* (History of the Kingdom of Naples) trans. Francis Frenaye, ed. H. Stuart Hughes (1925; reprint, Chicago: University of Chicago Press, 1971). Croce's work focuses on the political activity of the intelligensia and generally ignores broader social

history. Current Italian scholarship is only now uncovering the complicated processes and forces that acted to form Neapolitan culture. Raffaele Ajello, ed., *Storia di Napoli*, 11 vols., (Naples: Società editrice Storia di Napoli, 1967–78) has brought the best Neapolitan scholarship to bear on the city's history. For the history of Neapolitan humanism see Jerry H. Bentley, *Politics and Culture in Renaissance Naples* (Princeton, N.J.: Princeton University Press, 1987).

3. For a study of the communes and their relation to both the Neapolitan nobility and the law see Pierluigi Rovito, *Respublica dei togati: Giuristi e società nella Napoli dei seicento* (Naples: Jovene Editore, 1981), 231–89.

4. The issue that has never been resolved is just when Vico became overtly opposed to Cartesianism. See Nicolai Badaloni, *Introduzione a G. B. Vico* (Milan: Feltrinelli Editore, 1961) for a thorough account of the intellectual currents in Vico's milieu. See also Biagio Di Giovanni, "Il 'De nostri temporis studiorum ratione' nella cultura napoletana del primo settecento," in *Omaggio a Vico*, ed. Antonio Corsano et al. (Naples: Morano, 1968), 141–193, for an account of Vico's change in position. See also Fausto Nicolini, *La giovinezza di Giambattista Vico (1668–1700)* (Bari, 1932).

5. For a discussion of the *Investiganti*, see Badaloni, *Introduzione* 79–164 and Isoldi Jacobelli, *G.M. Vico: La vita e le opere* (Bologna: Cappelli, 1960), 61–63 and especially Max H.Fisch, "The Academy of the Investigators," *Science, Medicine, and History: Essays on the Evolution of Scientific Thought and Medical Practice Written in Honour of Charles Singer*, vol. 1, ed. E. A. Underwood (London: Oxford University Press, 1953), 521–63.

6. For an account of the Valletta circle, see Biagio di Giovanni, "Culture e vita in Giuseppe Valletta," *Studi sul settecento Italiano* (Naples: Instituto Italiano per gli Studi Storici, 1967). For an account of Shaftesbury's stay in Naples and his impact upon Neapolitan intellectual life, see Benedetto Croce, *Shaftesbury in Italy* (Cambridge: Cambridge University Press, 1926). Angus Fletcher also believes Vico and Shaftesbury had some direct contact. See "On the Syncretic Allegory of the *New Science*," *New Vico Studies* 4 (1986): 25–44. See also *Bibliographia Vichiana*, ed. Benedetto Croce, *accresciuta e rielaborata* Fausto Nicolino (Naples: Ricciardo Ricci, 1947).

7. The most recent accounts of the development of the Neapolitan legal "system" can be found in Pierluigi Rovito and Vittorio Sciuti Russi, *Astrea in Sicilia: Il ministerio togato nell società Siciliana dei secoli XVI e XVII* (Naples: Jovene Editore, 1983).

8. For a history of Spanish attempts to reform Neapolitan law and the court system see Rovito, *Respublica dei Togati*, 385–465.

9. For a study of D'Andrea's career and its impact on Neapolitan legal theory see Salvo Mastellone, *Francesco D'Andrea politico e giurista (1648–1698): L'Ascesa*

del ceto civile (Florence: 1969), and Nino Cortese, *I ricordi di un avvocato napolitano del seicento: Francesco D'Andrea* (Naples, 1923). For the relation of D'Andrea to DiCapua see Badaloni, *Introduzione,* 147–64.

10.   La negazione del *consensus gentium* come fonte di verità, operata da Descartes e poi da Hobbes, da Spinoza, da Pufendorf, da Bayle, da Locke, invalidava radicalmente quella *fictio* constituzionale su cui era fondati il diritto comune, e quindi, in una certa misura, tutto l'ordine costituito. Se il mirabile consenso di tutti popoli colti aveva confermato il valore assoluto dell '*Ordo* elaborato, sui fondamenti del diritto romano, dalla scienza giuridica tardo-medievale ed umanistica, negare la validità del *consensus* significava negare i fondamenti stessi della *respubblica,* e doversi affidare ad una ragion di Stato tendenzialmente libera da ogni *juris regula,* e quindi suscettibile di abombrare la tirannia: una prospettiva che non aveva preoccupato troppo Cola Capassa, ma che né Gravina, né Doria, né Vico avrebbero accettato senza riserve. (Raffaele Ajello, *Arcana juris: Diritto e politica nel settecento italiano* [Naples: Jovene Editore, 1976], 172–73.)

3   ORALITY AND *SENSUS COMMUNIS* IN VICO'S EARLY WRITINGS ON RHETORIC

1.   "On the Heroic Mind" (De mente eroica), trans. Elizabeth Sewell and Anthony C. Sirignano in *Vico and Contemporary Thought,* ed. Giorgio Tagliacozzo, Michael Mooney, and Donald P. Verene (Atlantic Highlands, N.J.: Humanities Press, 1976), 228–45.

2.   "Prudentia, quae saepe pro utilitate causarum artis praecepta deserit, et vel partes orationis transponit, ut si adversarii argumenta in animo iudicis fecerint impressionem, obiecta prius amoliamur."

3.   For an excellent treatment of the *sententia* and Vico's use of it see Michael Mooney, *Vico in the Tradition of Rhetoric* (Princeton, N.J.: Princeton University Press, 1985), 139–41 and 212f.

4.   For a discussion of the literary Baroque, see Lowry Nelson, Jr., "Baroque" and "Baroque Poetics," and William Van O'Connor, "Wit," in *Princeton Encyclopedia of Poetry and Poetics,* ed. Alex Preminger, Frank J. Warnke, and O. B. Hardison, Jr., 2d ed. (Princeton, N.J.: Princeton University Press, 1974), 66–71, 897–98.

5.   For a summary of the intellectual background of Vico's treatment of wit, see Mooney, *Vico in the Tradition,* 60–68. For a discussion of wit and *acutezze* in Baroque literary theory, see Giuseppe Conti, *La metafora barocca: Saggi sulle poetiche del seicento* (Milan: 1972); Benedetto Croce, *I trattatisti italiani del "concettismo" e Baltasar Gracian,* memoria letta all 'Accademia Pontiana (Na-

ples: A. Tessitore, 1899) and *Storia dell 'età barocca in Italia* (Bari: Laterza, 1929); and Joseph Mazzeo, *Renaissance and Seventeenth-Century Studies* (New York: Columbia University Press, 1964).

6. "Les pensées sont plus ou moins vraies, selon qu'elles sont plus ou moins conformes à leur objet. La conformité entière fait ce que nous apellons la justesse de la pensée, c'est à dire, que comme les habits sont justes quand ils viennent bien au corps, qu'ils sont tout à fait proportionnés à la personne qui les porte, les pensées sont justes aussi, quand elles conviennent parfaitement aux choses qu'elles représentent."

7. "Disons donc que les métaphores sont comme les voiles transparens, qui laissent voir ce qu'ils couvrent; ou comme des habits de masque, sous lesquels on reconnuît la personne qui est déguisée."

8. "Alterius speciei est ligamen, quod duas ideas conjungit, tertia mediante, hoc est ratione aliqua sive expressa, sive tacita; quod est tertium mentis nostrae opus, et dialecticis syllogismus, rhetoribus autem dicitur entimema."

9. "Acumen constituit in rara, et nova aptitudine duorum extremorum in aliquo dicto feliciter colligatorum. Eius autem inventio Aristotelis iudicio in poetica admodum difficilis est, ubi in argumento metaphorarum inquit: decenter uti translationibus maxime est arduum, nam non nisi versatilis ingenii est; et ut in rhetoricis habet, soli philosophi solertes, acutique praestare possunt, in rebus distantibus quid simile contemplari."

10. "Orator autem, acuto dicto prolato efficit pulchrum, quod ipsi auditori detegendum relinquit. Nam acuto dicto prolato, hoc est sub indicata ligaminis ratione auditor eam vestigat, medium invenit, extrema confert, aptitudinem contemplatur; et ipse detegit pulchrum, quot orator effecit: unde ipse sibi ingeniosus videtur, et acuto dicto non tam ut ab oratore prolato, quam ut a se intellecto delectatur."

11. "Argumentum autem est ratio aliunde desumpta, quae ad rem, qua de agitur, applicata, eam explicat. Id autem, unde ratio desumitur, dicitur locus. Locus igitur est argumenti domicilium, et sedes."

12. "Geometriam autem per formas ediscat, et una opera, et artem disponendi acquirat, et ipsius phantasiae ope, qua pueri plurimum volent, assuescat vera conficere."

13. "Et musica, quae practica dicitur, puerum imbutum velim, ut armonicas conformet aures, quae de numeris sive poeticis sive oratoris iudicant. . . ."

14. Vico's Latin reads "Critica est ars verae orationis, topica autem copiose." In *Opere di G. B. Vico,* Vol. 1 of 8, ed. Fausto Nicolini (Bari: Laterza, 1911–14), 82. Gianturco translates this as "Criticism is the art of true speech: *ars topica* of eloquence" (15).

15. "Numerorum enim tenuissima scientia est: et tenuia eloquentiae noxia . . ." (*Institutiones* 7).

16. "Ingenium sit ad excogitandum acutum, ut quam celerrime, et in rei, qua de agitur, medullas penetret, et omnia, quae ad rem spectant, circumspiciat, eique feliciter uniat. Idem sit ad explicandum facile, ut in sententiis res, in verbis sententiae pellucidus vitro perspiciantur . . ."

17. "Ingenii virtus . . . consistit in mutuo diversarum rerum ligamine: nam in acuto dicto haec tria inveniuntur, res, verba, et rerum verborumque ligamen."

4 SENSUS COMMUNIS IN THE NEW SCIENCE

1. The first part of *Il diritto universale,* the *De uno universi juris principio et fine uno,* was published in 1720, and the second part, *De constantia jurisprudentis,* was published in 1721.

2. Hugo Grotius, *De jure belli ac pacis,* Paris, 1625; Samuel Pufendorf, *De jure naturae et gentium,* 1672. For a study of Vico and Grotius, see Dario Faucci, "Vico and Grotius: Jurisconsults of Mankind," in *Giambattista Vico: An International Symposium,* ed. Giorgio Tagliacozzo and Hayden V. White (Baltimore: Johns Hopkins University Press, 1968), 61–76. For a study of Vico's significance as a legal thinker, see Elio Gianturco, "Vico's Significance in the History of Legal Thought," in ibid., 327–47.

3. For the relation of Roman law to Vico's thought see Max H. Fisch, "Vico on Roman Law," in *Essays in Political Theory: Presented to George H. Sabine,* ed. Milton R. Konwitz and Arthur E. Murphy (Ithaca, N.Y.: Cornell University Press, 1948), 62–88; Donald R. Kelley, "Vico's Road: From Philology to Jurisprudence—and back," in *Giambattista Vico's Science of Humanity,* ed. Giorgio Tagliacozzo and Donald P. Verene (Baltimore: Johns Hopkins University Press, 1976), 15–29; and Dino Pasini, *Diritto, società e stato in Vico* (Naples: Jovene, 1970).

4. Vico referred to the *jus gentium* as the "natural law of the gentes" in order to distinguish it from the Judaeo-Christian tradition where law is directly revealed by God.

5. For a study of how Vico used the *verum-certum* in his legal theory see Guido Fassò, *I "quattro auttori" del Vico: Saggio sulla genesi della "scienza nuova"* (Milan: Giuffrè, 1949).

6. Vico's anticipation of one of the central insights of post-structuralist criticism, the priority of writing, would make a tempting digression here, but the investigation of that insight will have to wait until chapter 6, where it will be considered along with his theory of metaphor. Here, it is only necessary to understand how Vico views the relation of language to the imaginative universal in each of the three ages.

5   *SENSUS COMMUNIS* IN VICO AND GADAMER

1. References are given to both the German text and the English translation of *Wahrheit und Methode.*
2. Vico himself never developed a hermeneutical theory in the contemporary sense of the term, nor am I attempting to develop a Vichian hermeneutics here. Rather I wish to use Vico heuristically to point out the essential weakness in Gadamer's hermeneutics that follows from his handling of Vico's idea of *sensus communis,* and second, to argue that any Vichian hermeneutics would have to remain true to Vico's oral, performative model of rhetoric. Emilio Betti has developed a hermeneutical theory that incorporates several Vichian ideas, for example, jurisprudence as a model of historical interpretation. But Betti differs with Vico on many key issues, for example, he denies any relation between *mythos* and *logos.* Much of Gadamer's work aims to refute Betti, and any attempt to "reconcile" Gadamer and Vico must begin by contrasting Gadamer and Betti. See Betti's *Hermeneutics as the General Methodology of the Geisteswissenschaften,* trans. Josef Bleicher; Joseph Bleicher, *Contemporary Hermeneutics: Hermeneutics as Method, Philosophy and Critique* (London: Routledge and Kegan Paul, 1980), 51–94; and Emilio Betti, *Teoria Generale della Interpretazione,* 2 vols. (Milan: Dott. A Giuffrè Editore, 1955).
3. See Max H. Fisch, "Vico on Roman Law," in *Essays in Political Theory Presented to George H. Sabine,* ed. Milton R. Konvitz and Arthur E. Murphy (Ithaca, N.Y.: Cornell University Press, 1948), 69 and Donald P. Verene, *Vico's Science of Imagination* (Ithaca, N.Y.: Cornell University Press, 1981), 179–80.

6   VICO AND DERRIDA ON LANGUAGE

1. For a comparison of Vico and Foucault, see Hayden White, *The Tropics of Discourse: Essays in Cultural Criticism* (Baltimore and London: Johns Hopkins University Press, 1978), 230–60, but see also John D. Schaeffer, "The Use and Misuse of Giambattista Vico: Rhetoric, Orality, and Theories of Discourse," in *The New Historicism,* ed. H. Aram Veeser (New York and London: Routledge and Kegan Paul, 1989), 89–101.

Bibliography

This list includes only those works cited in the running text.

Aquinas, Thomas. *Summa Theologica*. Editio Altera Romana. Rome: Forzani et S., 1894.

Ajello, Raffaele. *Arcana juris: Diritto e politica nel settecento italiano*. Naples: Jovene Editore, 1976

————. *Giuristi e società al tempo di Pietro Giannone*. Naples: Jovene Editore, 1980.

————, ed. *Storia di Napoli*. 11 vols. Naples: Società Editrice Storia di Napoli, 1967–78.

Amodeo, Frederico. *Le riforme* [sic] *universitaire di Carlo III e Ferdinando IV Borbone*. Naples, 1902.

Aristotle. *The Complete Works of Aristotle*. 2 vols. Edited by Jonathan Barnes. Bollingen Series, vol. 71, no. 2. Princeton, N.J.: Princeton University Press, 1984.

Arnauld, Antoine, and Pierre Nicole. *La Logique ou l'art de penser*. Edited by Pierre Clair and Francois Girbal. Paris: University Presses of France, 1965.

Augustine, Saint. *Confessions*. Translated by Vernon J. Bourke. Washington, D.C.: Catholic University Press of America, 1953.

————. *On Christian Doctrine (De Doctrina Christiana)*. Translated by D. W. Robertson. Indianapolis: Bobbs-Merrill, 1983.

Badaloni, Nicolai. *Introduzione a G. B. Vico*. Milan: Feltrinelli Editore, 1961.

Baldwin, Charles Sears. *Medieval Rhetoric and Poetic (to 1400)*. New York: Macmillan, 1928.

Beale, Walter H. *A Pragmatic Theory of Rhetoric*. Carbondale, Ill.: Southern Illinois University Press, 1987.

Beck, Frederick A. G. *Greek Education: 450–350 B.C.* London: Methuen, 1964.

Bernstein, Richard J. *Beyond Objectivism and Relativism: Science, Hermeneutics and Praxis*. Philadelphia: University of Pennsylvania Press, 1983.

Bleicher, Joseph. *Contemporary Hermeneutics: Hermeneutics as Method, Philosophy and Critique*. London: Routledge and Kegan Paul, 1980.

Bonner, Stanley F. *Education in Ancient Rome: From the Elder Cato to the Younger Pliny*. Berkeley: University of California Press, 1977.

Bouhours, Dominique. *La manière de bien penser dans les ouvrages d'esprit.* Paris: Libraire Associés, 1771.

Bouwsma, William J. *Venice and the Defense of Republican Liberty: Renaissance Values in the Age of the Counter-Reformation.* Berkeley: University of California Press, 1968.

Brucker, Gene. *The Civil World of Early Renaissance Florence.* Princeton, N.J.: Princeton University Press, 1977.

Burckhardt, Jacob. *The Civilization of the Renaissance in Italy.* Translated by S. G. C. Middlemore. Revised and edited by Irene Gordon. New York: New American Library, 1960.

Butler, Eliza M. *The Tyranny of Greece over Germany: A Study of the Influence Exercised by Greek Art and Poetry over the Great German Writers of the 18th, 19th and 20th Centuries.* Boston: Beacon Press, 1958.

Cicero, Marcus Tullius. *De Oratore.* 2 vols. Translated by E. W. Sutton and H. Rackham. Cambridge, Mass.: Harvard University Press; London: Heinemann, 1979.

———. *De Partitione Oratoria.* Translated by H. Rackham. Cambridge, Mass.: Harvard University Press; London: Heinemann, 1943.

———. *Topica.* Translated by H. M. Hubbell. Cambridge, Mass.: Harvard University Press; London: Heinemann, 1949.

Coers, Kathy Frashure. "Vico and MacIntyre." *New Vico Studies* 4 (1986): 131–33.

Croce, Benedetto. *History of the Kingdom of Naples.* Translated by Francis Frenaye. Edited by H. Stuart Hughes. Chicago: University of Chicago Press, 1971.

———. *Shaftesbury in Italy.* Cambridge: Cambridge University Press, 1923.

de Dainville, Francois. *L'Éducation des Jésuites (XVI–XVIIIe siecle).* Paris: Les Editions de Minuit, 1978.

Derrida, Jacques. *Dissemination.* Translated by Barbara Johnson. Chicago: University of Chicago Press, 1981.

———. *Of Grammatology.* Translated by Gayatri C. Spivak. Baltimore: Johns Hopkins University Press, 1976.

———. "Signature Event Context." Translated by Samuel Weber and Jeffrey Mehlman. *Glyph One.* Johns Hopkins Textual Studies, 172–97. Baltimore: Johns Hopkins University Press, 1977.

———. "White Mythology: Metaphor in the Text of Philosophy." Translated by F. C. T. Moore. *New Literary History* 6 (1974): 5–74.

Dumitri, Anton. *History of Logic.* 4 vols. Tunbridge Wells: Abacus Press, 1977.

Erasmus, Desiderius. *Adagiorum.* Edited by Felix Heinimann and Emanuel Kienzle. *Opera Omnia.* Vol. II, parts 4–6. Amsterdam: North-Holland, 1981–87.

———. *On Copia of Words and Ideas* (De utraque verborum ac rerum copia).

Translated by Donald B. King and H. David Rix. Milwaukee: Marquette University Press, 1963.

————. *The Colloquies of Erasmus*. Translated by Craig Thompson. Chicago: University of Chicago Press, 1965.

Farrell, Allen P. *The Jesuit Code of Liberal Education: Development and Scope of the Ratio Studiorum*. Milwaukee: Bruce, 1938.

Fassò, Guido. "The Problem of Law and the Historical Origin of the *New Science*." In *Giambattista Vico's Science of Humanity*, edited by Giorgio Tagliacozzo and Donald P. Verene, 3–14. Baltimore: Johns Hopkins University Press, 1976.

Fitzpatrick, Edward A. *St. Ignatius and the Ratio Studiorum*. New York: McGraw-Hill, 1933.

France, Peter. *Rhetoric and Truth in France: Descartes to Diderot*. Oxford: Clarendon Press, 1972.

Funkenstein, Amos. "Natural Science and Social Theory: Hobbes, Spinoza and Vico." In *Vico's Science of Humanity*, edited by Giorgio Tagliacozzo and Donald P. Verene, 187–212, Baltimore: Johns Hopkins University Press, 1976.

Gadamer, Hans Georg. "*Rhetorik, Hermeneutik und Ideologiekritik: Metakritische Erörterungen zu Wahrheit und Methode*." In *Hermeneutik und Ideologiekritik*, edited by K. O. Apel et al. Frankfurt: Suhrkamp, 1971.

————. *Truth and Method*. Translated and edited by Garrett Barden and John Cumming. New York: Seabury Press, 1975; published in German as *Wahrheit und Methode: Grundzüge einer philosophischen Hermeneutik*. 2d ed. Tubingen: J. C. B. Mohr (Paul Siebeck), 1965.

Galasso, Giuseppe. "*Napoli al tempo di Vico*": *Giambattista Vico nel terzo centenario della nascita*. Naples: Edizione Scientifiche Italiane, 1971.

Gilby, Thomas O. P. *Barbara Celarent: A Description of Scholastic Dialectic*. London: Longmans Green, 1949.

Gilson, Etienne. *Elements of Christian Philosophy*. Westport, Conn.: Greenwood Press, 1978.

Di Giovanni, Biagio. "*Il 'de nostri temporis studiorum ratione' nella cultural napoletana del primo settecento*": *Omaggio a Vico*. Edited by Antonio Corsano et al., 143–91. Naples: Morano, 1968.

————. "*Scienza e vita civile*": *Storia di Napoli*, vol. 6. Edited by Raffaele Ajello, 421–42. Naples: Società Editrice di Storia di Napoli, 1967–78.

Gleijeses, Vittorio. *La Storia di Napoli dalle origini ai nostri giorni*. 3d ed. Naples: Società Editrice Napoletana, 1977.

Grassi, Ernesto. *Rhetoric as Philosophy: The Humanist Tradition*. University Park, Pa.: Pennsylvania State University Press, 1980.

Habermas, Jürgen. *Erkenntnis und Interesse*. Frankfurt: Suhrkamp, 1968.

————. "The Hermeneutic Claim to Universality." Translated by Joseph Bleicher. In *Contemporary Hermeneutics: Method, Philosophy and Critique*, edited by Joseph Bleicher, 181–211. London: Routledge and Kegan Paul, 1980.

Havelock, Eric. *Preface to Plato.* Cambridge, Mass.: Harvard University Press, 1963.

Henry, D. P. *Medieval Logic and Metaphysics: A Modern Introduction.* London: Hutchinson University Library, 1972.

Hinman, Lawrence M. "Quid Facti or Quid Juris? The Fundamental Ambiguity of Gadamer's Understanding of Hermeneutics." *Philosophy and Phenomonological Research* 40 (1980): 512–35.

Jacobelli, Isoldi, G. B. *Vico: La vita e le opere.* Bologna: Cappelli, 1960.

Jaeger, Werner. *Paideia: The Ideals of Greek Culture.* Vol. 1, 2d ed. Translated by Gilbert Highet. New York: Oxford University Press, 1965.

Kennedy, George. *The Art of Persuasion in Greece.* Princeton, N.J.: Princeton University Press, 1963.

———. *The Art of Rhetoric in the Roman World: 300 B.C.–A.D. 300.* Princeton, N.J.: Princeton University Press, 1972.

———. *Greek Rhetoric Under Christian Emperors.* Princeton, N.J.: Princeton University Press, 1983.

Krois, John Michael. "Vico's and Pierce's *Sensus Communis.*" In *Vico: Past and Present,* edited by Giorgio Tagliacozzo, 58–71. Atlantic Highlands, N.J.: Humanities Press, 1981.

Lancelot, Claude. *Grammaire générale et raisonée de Port-Royal.* Geneva: Slatkine Reprints, 1968.

Lanham, Richard A. *Literacy and the Survival of Humanism.* New Haven, Conn.: Yale University Press, 1983.

Lord, Albert. *The Singer of Tales.* Harvard Studies in Comparative Literature, vol. 24. Cambridge, Mass.: Harvard University Press, 1960.

MacIntyre, Alasdair. *After Virtue.* Notre Dame, Ind.: University of Notre Dame Press, 1981.

———. *Whose Justice? Which Rationality?* Notre Dame, Ind.: University of Notre Dame Press, 1988.

McKeon, Richard. "Rhetoric in the Middle Ages." In *The Province of Rhetoric,* edited by Joseph Schwartz and John A. Rycenga, 172–212. New York: Ronald Press, 1965.

Mauro, Tullio de. "Giambattista Vico: From Rhetoric to Linguistic Historicism." In *Giambattista Vico: An International Symposium,* edited by Giorgio Tagliacozzo and Hayden V. White, 279–95. Baltimore: Johns Hopkins University Press, 1969.

Mazzeo, Joseph. *Renaissance and Seventeenth-Century Studies.* New York: Columbia University Press, 1964.

Mooney, Michael. *Vico in the Tradition of Rhetoric.* Princeton, N.J.: Princeton University Press, 1985.

Muir, Edward. *Civic Ritual in Renaissance Venice*. Princeton, N.J.: Princeton University Press, 1981.

Muller, Gregor. *Bildung und erziehung in humanismus der italienischen renaissance*. Wiesbaden: Franz Steiner, 1969.

Murphy, James J. *Rhetoric in the Middle Ages: A History of Rhetorical Theory from St. Augustine to the Renaissance*. Berkeley: University of California Press, 1974.

Ong, Walter J. *Orality and Literacy: The Technologizing of the Word*. New York: Methuen, 1982.

————. *Ramus, Method and the Decay of Dialogue*. Cambridge, Mass.: Harvard University Press, 1958.

————. *Rhetoric, Romance and Technology: Studies in the Interaction of Expression and Culture*. Ithaca, N.Y.: Cornell University Press, 1971.

Parry, Milman. *The Making of Homeric Verse: The Collected Papers of Milman Parry*. Edited by Adam Parry. Oxford: Clarendon Press, 1971.

————. ed. *Serbocroatian Heroic Songs*. Translated by Albert B. Lord. Cambridge, Mass.: Harvard University Press; Belgrade: Serbian Academy of Sciences, 1954.

Phillips, Margaret Mann. *The Adages of Erasmus: A Study with Translations*. Cambridge: Cambridge University Press, 1964.

Pompa, Leon. *Vico: A Study of the "New Science"*. Cambridge: Cambridge University Press, 1975.

Quintillian. *The Institutio Oratoria of Quintillian*. 4 vols. Translated by H. E. Butler. Cambridge, Mass.: Harvard University Press; London: Heinemann, 1980.

Roberts, J. W. *City of Sokrates: An Introduction to Classical Athens*. London: Routledge and Kegan Paul, 1984.

Rorty, Richard. *Philosophy and the Mirror of Nature*. Princeton, N.J.: Princeton University Press, 1979.

Rovito, Pierluigi. *Respublica dei togati: Giuristi e società nella Napoli dei seicento*. Naples: Jovene Editore, 1981.

Saussure, Ferdinand de. *Course in General Linguistics*. Edited by Charles Bally and Albert Sechehaye. Translated by Wade Baskin. New York: McGraw-Hill, 1966.

Shaftesbury, Third Earl of. *Characteristicks of Men, Manners, Opinion, Times*. 3 vols., 2d ed. 1714. Reprint. Hantsford, Eng: Gregg International, 1968.

Siegel, Jerrold E. *Rhetoric and Philosophy in Renaissance Humanism: The Union of Eloquence and Wisdom, Petrarch to Valla*. Princeton, N.J.: Princeton University Press, 1968.

Solmsen, Frederick. "Notes on Aristotle's *Rhetoric*." In *The Province of Rhetoric*, edited by Joseph Schwartz and John A. Rycenga, 128–36. New York: Ronald Press, 1965.

Torraca, Francesco. *Storia della Università di Napoli,* edited by Ricardo Ricciardi. Naples, 1924.

Verene, Donald P. *Vico's Science of Imagination.* Ithaca, N.Y.: Cornell University Press, 1981.

Vico, Giambattista. *The Autobiography of Giambattista Vico.* Translated by Max H. Fisch and Thomas G. Bergin. Ithaca, N.Y.: Cornell University Press, 1944.

———. *De antiquissima italorum sapientia ex linguae latinae originibus eruenda (Vico: Selected Writings).* Edited and translated by Leon Pompa. Cambridge: Cambridge University Press, 1982.

———. *Institutiones oratoriae.* vol. 7, *Opere complete.* Edited by Giuseppe Ferrari. Naples: Presso I Fratelli Morano, 1865.

———. *The New Science of Giambattista Vico.* Translated by Thomas G. Bergin and Max H. Frisch. Ithaca, N.Y.: Cornell University Press, 1944.

———. *On the Heroic Mind* (De mente eroica). Translated by Elizabeth Sewell and Anthony C. Sirignano. Vol. 2 of *Vico and Contemporary Thought* (2 vols. in 1), edited by Michael Mooney, Giorgio Tagliacozzo, and Donald P. Verene, 228–45. Atlantic Highlands, N.J.: Humanities Press, 1976.

———. *On the Study Methods of Our Time* (De nostri temporis studiorum ratione). Translated by Elio Gianturco. Indianapolis: Library of the Liberal Arts; Bobbs-Merrill, 1965.

Voitle, Robert. *The Third Earl of Shaftesbury 1671–1713.* Baton Rouge: Louisiana State University Press, 1984.

———. "Shaftesbury's Moral Sense." *Studies in Philology* 52 (1955): 17–38.

Warnke, Georgia. *Gadamer: Hermeneutics, Tradition and Reason.* Stanford, Calif.: Stanford University Press, 1987.

Weaver, Richard M. *The Ethics of Rhetoric.* South Bend, Ind.: Regnery/Gateway, 1953.

Webster, T. B. L. *Athenian Culture and Society.* Berkeley: University of California Press, 1973.

Weinsheim, Joel C. *Gadamer's Hermeneutics: A Reading of Truth and Method.* New Haven, Conn.: Yale University Press, 1985.

Williams, Bernard. *Ethics and the Limits of Philosophy.* London: Fontana Press/Collins, 1985.

Woodward, William. *Desiderius Erasmus Concerning the Aim and Method of Education.* Classics in Education, no. 19. New York: Teachers College, Columbia University, 1904. Reprint 1964.

———. *Vittorina da Feltre and Other Humanist Educators.* 2d ed. Classics in Education, no. 18. New York: Teachers College, Columbia University, 1897. Reprint 1963.

Index

Acuity: in Aristotle, 66; in metaphor, 73, 74. See also *Acutezze;* Metaphor; Wit

Acutezze, 63, 74

Aesthetics, 74, 143

Ages of man, three, 92–98

Aisthesis idia, 103

Ajello, Raffael, 47, 49, 51–52

Aletheia, 131, 133

Alfonso of Aragon, king of Naples, 36

Analogy, perception of, 73

D'Andrea, Francesco, 51

Aquinas, Saint Thomas, 2, 101, 104, 105, 113, 155

Arche, 87, 91, 98, 120, 125, 134, 135, 142, 148, 159, 160

Arendt, Hannah, 153

Aristotle, 24, 30, 31, 58, 102, 104, 106, 112–13, 131, 132; *De Anima*, 2, 101, 103; definition of *sensus communis*, 83; *dispositio* in, 59; ethics, 155, 156; *Organon*, 51; *Poetics*, 65, 66; *Politics*, 156; "proportional metaphor" in, 62, 63, 65; *Rhetoric*, 15–17, 57, 61, 62, 65, 66, 156; *Topics*, 142

Arnaud, Antoine, 32

Ars dictaminis, 24

Ars poetriae, 24

Ars praedicandi, 23, 24

Ars topica, 71

Athens, 12, 13, 15

Augustine, Saint, 22–23, 156; *Confessions*, 23; *De doctrina christiana*, 22, 23

Auliso, Domenico, 41

Baldwin, C. S., 22

Baron, Hans, 27

Baroque, 34, 61, 63, 133; aesthetics, 143; notion of metaphor, 91; painting, 74

Bayle, Pierre, 52

Beale, Walter H., 157

Berkeley, George, 3

Bernstein, Richard, 4, 111, 113, 123, 153, 156

Boileau-Despréaux, Nicolas, 128

Bon sens, 1, 32, 55, 58, 72, 160

Bonner, Stanley F., 18

Bouhours, Doninique, 63, 64, 74; on metaphor, 64, 128, 130, 135

Burckhardt, Jacob, 36

Butler, Eliza, 125–26

Capasso, Cola, 52

Capitalism, 118

D'Capua, Leonardo, 51

Cartesianism, 1, 58, 130, 132, 160; method and logic in, 71; in Neapolitan legal reform, 51–53; "rhetorical," 52; at the University of Naples, 40; Vico's attack on, 54, 78; virtue in, 155. *See also* Descartes, René

Castiglione, Baldassare, 55, 158

Catholic Church: in Naples, 37

Christianity, 22

Cicero, 12, 23, 24, 110; *inventio* in, 57, 59; and Jesuit education, 30, 32; in the Renaissance, 26, 27, 28; and Vico, 60, 66–67

Civilization: and rhetoric, 147

Classic, the: concept of, 108–9; status of, 114; truth of, 115

Coers, Kathy, 155

About the Author

John D. Schaeffer is Associate Professor of English at Columbus College, Georgia.

Library of Congress Cataloging-in-Publication Data
Schaeffer, John D.
Sensus communis : Vico, rhetoric, and the limits of relativism/
by John D. Schaeffer
Includes bibliographical references.
ISBN 0-8223-1026-0
1. Vico, Giambattista, 1668–1744. 2. Common sense—History.
3. Rhetoric. 4. Hermeneutics—History. 5. Languages—Philosophy—
History. I. Title.
B3583.S33 1990
195—dc20 89-23826 CIP